Pathways

LESSONS FROM ESTHER

From Providence to Purpose

TONY EVANS

LifeWay Press®
Nashville, Tennessee

EDITORIAL TEAM

Heather Hair
Writer

Reid Patton
Content Editor

David Haney
Production Editor

Jon Rodda
Art Director

Joel Polk
Editorial Team Leader

Brian Daniel
Manager, Short-Term Discipleship

Michael Kelley
Director, Discipleship and Groups Ministry

Published by LifeWay Press® • © 2018 Tony Evans

ISBN 978-1-4627-9679-3 • Item 005802343

Dewey decimal classification: 248.84
Subject headings: ESTHER, QUEEN / PROVIDENCE AND GOVERNMENT OF GOD / CHRISTIAN LIFE

My deepest thanks go to Mrs. Heather Hair for her skills and insights in collaboration on this manuscript.

Passage summaries in the "Start" sections of all group sessions are adapted from David S. Dockery, gen. ed., *Concise Bible Commentary* (Nashville: B&H Publishing Group, 2010).

To order additional copies of this resource, write to LifeWay Resources Customer Service; One LifeWay Plaza; Nashville, TN 37234; fax 615-251-5933; call toll free 800-458-2772; order online at LifeWay.com; email orderentry@lifeway.com; or visit the LifeWay Christian Store serving you.

Printed in the United States of America

Groups Ministry Publishing • LifeWay Resources • One LifeWay Plaza • Nashville, TN 37234

Contents

About the Author

DR. TONY EVANS is one of America's most respected leaders in evangelical circles. He's a pastor, a best-selling author, and a frequent speaker at Bible conferences and seminars throughout the nation. He has served as the senior pastor of Oak Cliff Bible Fellowship for more than forty years, witnessing its growth from ten people in 1976 to more than ten thousand congregants with more than one hundred ministries.

Dr. Evans also serves as the president of The Urban Alternative, a national ministry that seeks to restore hope and transform lives through the proclamation and application of God's Word. His daily radio broadcast, *The Alternative with Dr. Tony Evans*, can be heard on more than 1,300 radio outlets throughout the United States and in more than 130 countries.

Dr. Evans holds the honor of writing and publishing the first full-Bible commentary and study Bible by an African-American. A former chaplain for the Dallas Cowboys, he's currently the chaplain for the NBA's Dallas Mavericks, a team he has served for more than thirty years.

Through his local church and national ministry, Dr. Evans has set in motion a kingdom-agenda philosophy of ministry that teaches God's comprehensive rule over every area of life, as demonstrated through the individual, family, church, and society.

Dr. Evans is married to Lois, his wife and ministry partner of more than forty years. They are the proud parents of four—Chrystal, Priscilla, Anthony Jr., and Jonathan—and have a number of grandchildren.

Introduction and Background

THE MESSAGE OF ESTHER

Esther is unique because it's the only book in Scripture that doesn't directly mention the name of God. God ordained this omission because He wanted to use the book to show the way His providence (that is, His invisible hand) works behind the scenes to bring about His purposes in history. So even though God isn't on the pages of Esther, His fingerprints appear throughout the book.

At times the book seems rather secular; historically, this fact has contributed to questions about its place in the canon of the synagogue and the church. Esther is tightly connected with specific historical events, yet it's also a piece of literature, a narrative with all of the literary features needed to make it a great story. Its purposes aren't always explicitly stated but are derived from the story as a whole.

Esther's dramatic story unfolds with the people of God, the Jews, living in Persia, where God had exiled them because of their sin. Through a series of circumstances, the young Jewish woman for whom the book is named was selected as the new queen because of her natural beauty. Her people were then threatened with annihilation by the hand of an evil man named Haman. But God, working behind the scenes, brought about His people's deliverance when Esther decided to risk her life by speaking to the king for them. She sealed her resolve with the words "If I perish, I perish" (4:16).

The Book of Esther demonstrates that although His methods vary, God is in control. His kingdom promises and purposes can't be thwarted.

CIRCUMSTANCES OF WRITING

———

AUTHOR. As with many Old Testament books, the author of the Book of Esther is unknown. The book itself names no writer, and no reliable tradition exists that identifies one.

The Jewish Talmud suggests that the members of the Great Synagogue wrote the book. However, it's hard to imagine that this prestigious group of religious scholars write a book that mentions the Persian king 190 times but never mentions God. Many early writers, Jewish as well as Christian, suggested Mordecai as the author.

BACKGROUND. In 587 BC Jerusalem fell to King Nebuchadnezzar, who carried many of the people of Judah into exile in Babylon (see 2 Chron. 36:15-21). In 539 BC Cyrus the Great, the ruler of the Medo-Perisan Empire, conquered Babylon and issued a decree permitting exiled people, including the Jews, to return to their homelands (see 2 Chron. 36:22-23). Although many Jews returned, others continued to live throughout the Medo-Persian Empire. The events in the Book of Esther took place during the reign of King Ahasuerus (Xerxes I), who ruled the empire from 486 to 465 BC. His son, Artaxerxes I, would later send both Ezra and Nehemiah to Jerusalem (see Ezra 7:11-28; Neh 2:1-8).

KEY THEMES

———

HOPE. For the Jewish people scattered around the Persian Empire, the Book of Esther gave encouragement and hope. It provided a model for how the Jewish people could not only survive but also thrive in a Gentile environment. It showed how Jewish people could effectively serve in positions of high responsibility while maintaining their Jewish identity and their commitment to the God of Israel. It showed how Jewish leaders could be used to bring blessing to their Gentile rulers and neighbors. And for a people far from the land of their forefathers, it demonstrated that the God of Israel was still able to redeem His people in their oppression, whether they were in Egypt, Israel, or Persia.

DIVINE PROVIDENCE. It's unlikely that the lack of any mention of God in the Book of Esther is accidental. It leaves the reader to ponder the work of God, evident but unseen, in the unfolding story of deliverance and redemption. This approach is fitting because Jews in exile would be tempted to find a lack of evidence for God's overt presence to be evidence for His actual absence. The Book of Esther counters this notion, depicting God's providence as ruling even the events of foreign lands during the Jews' exile.

GOD'S UNLIKELY INSTRUMENTS. Part of the mystery of God's providence in the book is how God can use unlikely people to help accomplish His plans. Who would ever guess that a young Jewish woman named Esther, an orphan, would end up being the queen of the greatest empire the world had ever known? Who but God could bring about such a powerful reversal through a young woman?

CONTRIBUTION TO THE BIBLE

———

Without ever mentioning God directly, the Book of Esther underscores the providence of God. God's promise to give the Jews an eternal ruler remained in place, even in the face of threatened annihilation. Esther shows us that many Jews remained faithful to their God even in exile. They kept their identity as God's people through the synagogues that developed as the centers of the Jewish community wherever Jews settled. The synagogues would later play a significant role as the gospel spread throughout the Roman Empire, for these served as natural starting places for the deliverance of the gospel in the towns visited by the apostles (for example, see Acts 9:20; 17:1-2; 18:19; 19:8).[1]

---

1. Adapted from CSB Study Bible (Nashville: Holman Bible Publishers, 2017) and from Tony Evans Study Bible (Nashville: Holman Bible Publishers, 2019).

How to Get the Most from This Study

This Bible study book includes six weeks of content for group and personal study.

BACKGROUND INFORMATION

Helpful background information about the Book of Esther can be found on pages 5–7.

GROUP SESSIONS

Regardless of what day of the week your group meets, each week of content begins with the group session. Each group session uses the following format to facilitate simple yet meaningful interaction among group members, with God's Word, and with the teaching of Dr. Evans.

START. This page includes questions to get the conversation started and to introduce the video teaching.

WATCH. This page includes key points from Dr. Evans's teaching, along with blanks for taking notes as participants watch the video.

RESPOND. This page includes questions and statements that guide the group to respond to Dr. Evans's video teaching and to relevant Bible passages.

PERSONAL STUDY

Each week provides five days of Bible study and learning activities for individual engagement between group sessions. The personal study revisits stories, Scriptures, and themes Dr. Evans introduced in the videos so that participants can understand and apply them on a personal level. The days are numbered 1–5 to provide personal reading and activities for each day of the week, leaving two days off to worship with your church family and to meet as a small group. If your group meets on the same day as your worship gathering, use the extra day to reflect on what God is teaching you and to practice putting the biblical principles into action.

Tips for Leading a Small Group

Follow these guidelines to prepare for each group session.

PRAYERFULLY PREPARE

REVIEW. Review the weekly material and group questions ahead of time.

PRAY. Be intentional about praying for each person in the group.

Ask the Holy Spirit to work through you and the group discussion as you point to Jesus each week through God's Word.

MINIMIZE DISTRACTIONS

Create a comfortable environment. If group members are uncomfortable, they'll be distracted and therefore not engaged in the group experience. Plan ahead by considering these details:

SEATING
TEMPERATURE
LIGHTING
FOOD OR DRINK
SURROUNDING NOISE
GENERAL CLEANLINESS

At best, thoughtfulness and hospitality show guests and group members they're welcome and valued in whatever environment you choose to gather. At worst, people may never notice your effort, but they're also not distracted. Do everything in your ability to help people focus on what's most important: connecting with God, with the Bible, and with one another.

INCLUDE OTHERS

Your goal is to foster a community in which people are welcome just as they are but encouraged to grow spiritually. Always be aware of opportunities to include any people who visit the group and to invite new people to join your group.

An inexpensive way to make first-time guests feel welcome or to invite someone to get involved is to give them their own copies of this Bible-study book.

ENCOURAGE DISCUSSION

A good small-group experience has the following characteristics.

EVERYONE PARTICIPATES. Encourage everyone to ask questions, share responses, or read aloud.

NO ONE DOMINATES—NOT EVEN THE LEADER. Be sure that your time speaking as a leader takes up less than half of your time together as a group. Politely guide discussion if anyone dominates.

NOBODY IS RUSHED THROUGH QUESTIONS. Don't feel that a moment of silence is a bad thing. People often need time to think about their responses to questions they've just heard or to gain courage to share what God is stirring in their hearts.

INPUT IS AFFIRMED AND FOLLOWED UP. Make sure you point out something true or helpful in a response. Don't just move on. Build community with follow-up questions, asking how other people have experienced similar things or how a truth has shaped their understanding of God and the scripture you're studying. People are less likely to speak up if they fear that you don't actually want to hear their answers or that you're looking for only a certain answer.

GOD AND HIS WORD ARE CENTRAL. Opinions and experiences can be helpful, but God has given us the truth. Trust God's Word to be the authority and God's Spirit to work in people's lives. You can't change anyone, but God can. Continually point people to the Word and to active steps of faith.

KEEP CONNECTING

Think of ways to connect with group members during the week. Participation during the group session is always improved when members spend time connecting with one another outside the group sessions. The more people are comfortable with and involved in one another's lives, the more they'll look forward to being together. When people move beyond being friendly to truly being friends who form a community, they come to each session eager to engage instead of merely attending.

Encourage group members with thoughts, commitments, or questions from the session by connecting through these communication channels:

EMAILS
TEXTS
SOCIAL MEDIA

When possible, build deeper friendships by planning or spontaneously inviting group members to join you outside your regularly scheduled group time for activities like these:

MEALS
FUN ACTIVITIES
PROJECTS AROUND YOUR HOME, CHURCH, OR COMMUNITY

Week 1

THE SECURITY
OF SOVEREIGNTY

Start

Welcome to group session 1 of Pathways.

For the next six weeks we're going to study the Book of Esther. Have you ever studied this book personally or with a group? What do you know about the Book of Esther? What are looking forward to during this study?

Esther is a kind of Cinderella story. Why do these stories resonate with us?

**Before we begin, read aloud Esther 1:1–2:18 together as a group.
The passage is summarized below.**

King Ahasuerus convened a royal reception in his third year on the throne (483 BC). The assembly he called lasted 180 days, and it culminated in a 7-day feast of luxurious dining and drunkenness. Esther 1:1-7 describes the opulence of the Persian court to indicate the vast resources and power of the king.

In a drunken stupor the king called for Queen Vashti "to display her beauty" (v. 11) before his guests. Her refusal, probably out of decency, threatened the king's reputation, and Ashasuerus banished her.

After four years the king became lonely and sought a new wife. Esther was among the young women brought to the king's palace because of her exceptional beauty. Esther won his approval and became queen. Mordecai, Esther's elder cousin who had raised her, advised her to conceal her nationality.

Watch

Complete this viewer guide as you watch video session 1.

The Bible has sixty-six books. Sixty-five of them mention the name of God.

Esther was placed in the Bible because God wanted to show all of us something about His character and methodology when He is not overtly being seen.

The Book of Esther is set between chapters 6 and 7 of the Book of Ezra.

According to the laws of the Medes and the Persians, when a law was set, it could not be changed.

God takes natural things that He has given us and, through the streams of meandering, positions them for opportunity in order to fulfill His sovereign purpose.

You're part of something much bigger. It's not just about what's happening today. It's about what God has promised, in His sovereign plan, to do, His will that He is determined to accomplish.

God can hit a bull's-eye with a crooked stick.

Providence ought to give you hope that even if things aren't perfect, it doesn't have to be the end of the story.

Discuss

Discuss the video with your group, using the following questions.

As you read Esther 1:1–2:18 and heard Dr. Evans's teaching, what stood out to you?

One reason Esther is such a beloved, enduring book is that it's an excellent story. What elements of a good story do we see in these opening chapters?

Dr. Evans said God often "zigzags us to our purpose." When has God taken you on an indirect path to accomplish His will in your life? How did you respond to the twists and turns?

What did you learn on the indirect path that you might not have learned on a more direct one?

According to Dr. Evans, why doesn't the Book of Esther mention the name of God? Why should the seeming absence of God's name in this story actually encourage us when it seems as if God isn't with us?

God used Esther's physical beauty to draw the attention of the king. How does God use our natural talents and ability to further His providence? What's an example from your own life?

Dr. Evans mentioned that a few sins were involved in the process by which Esther became a queen. Although Esther's becoming the queen was part of God's plan, the sin wasn't. How does God providentially accomplish His will despite human sin?

Esther was unaware that she was part of God's divine plan. In what ways is God's providence a reason for hope?

Read week 1 and complete the activities before the next group session.

The Security of Sovereignty

Have you ever wondered why you're where you are and when things are going to change? That's a question we all face at some point in our lives. If you haven't asked it yet, just wait. I have a feeling you might.

God rarely takes us directly from point A to point B on this pathway called life. Rather, He typically has us travel a winding road made up of twists and turns, detours and traffic jams. Why? Because unlike human beings, who can see the present and only guess at the future, God is an infinite being who isn't bound by time. He knows the end from the beginning (see Isa. 46:10). He connects the future with the past. The bottom line is that God knows the right path to take you exactly where He wants you to be. He does this with His providential hand.

My hope for this Bible study is that as you and your small group, family, or friends complete the daily readings and activities, you'll learn to discover the power of God's providence in the midst of your personal pain, fear, gain, loss, and love. In addition, I want you to discover the very personal nature of God as He maneuvers each of us along multiple pathways, intersecting what and whom He wishes according to His intended aim.

Over the next six weeks you'll learn to recognize God's providential hand through the biblical Book of Esther. It's the story of how God took a young Jewish exile named Esther, made her queen of Persia, and used her to deliver His people from the threat of destruction.

This short book, tucked in the middle of the Old Testament, never mentions the covenant name of Yahweh. Yet behind the scenes, in the minutiae and details, in every choice and decision, God sovereignly guided the events of Esther to His chosen outcome. As we read Esther, we'll see two foundational ideas that illuminate God's character: His sovereignty and His providence.

God is the greatest storyteller. He's the puppet master behind the scenes. When you learn how to locate Him in what appears to be His absence, you'll learn to trust Him along the dark pathways life often presents. Then you'll be perfectly positioned on your own unique pathway to purpose. On this path you'll discover in what ways you too have been created for God's purpose and have been placed in your own spectacular story, like the royal Esther, for such a time as this.

This week's teaching draws out themes found in Esther 1:1–2:18. Review this passage of Scripture before beginning your personal study.

⊙ DAY 1 ⊙

WORRIED YOU'RE NOT ON THE RIGHT PATH?

Have you ever felt that you were on the wrong path? Have you ever surveyed the circumstances of your life and been unable to find God in them? This may seem like an odd way to begin a Bible study, but taking a moment to consider these questions will help you begin your study of *Pathways*.

As we consider the Book of Esther in depth during the coming weeks, you'll undoubtedly notice that God seems conspicuously absent. While the king of Persia is mentioned 190 times, the name of God never appears. The further we venture in the book, the more the circumstances will seem to be stacked against Esther. Yet when it seems as though Esther is on the wrong path, the invisible hand of God is always at work. The story of Esther urges us to trust God even when we're worried that we're not on the right path. Here at the beginning of our time together, let's take a moment to address that concern.

How do you respond when you feel that your life isn't going the way you hoped or planned?

Even though this is a common struggle, why is it such a difficult struggle?

If we were honest, we'd admit that we've all struggled with questions and doubts, wondering why God has taken us where He has or allowed us to face what we were facing. It's human to feel these emotions. It's human to lose hope. You don't need to pretend that you're superspiritual. God has seen discouragement and doubt before. He knows our frame. He knows we're modified dust (Ps. 103:14).

In those times we just want God to show up to let us know He's still there. We reach for Him, but like the wind, He escapes our grasp. His invisible hand eludes us, while His words urge us to keep walking the path He has called us to take.

But do we take the next step? Do we walk in faith? Are we able to believe the words spoken through the prophet Isaiah?

> *Do not fear, for I have redeemed you;*
> *I have summoned you by name; you are mine.*
> *When you pass through the waters,*
> *I will be with you;*
> *and when you pass through the rivers,*
> *they will not sweep over you.*
> *When you walk through the fire,*
> *you will not be burned;*
> *the flames will not set you ablaze.*
> *For I am the* LORD *your God,*
> *the Holy One of Israel, your Savior.*
> ISAIAH 43:1-3, NIV

A prophet may not show up at our door with a message from the Lord, but God has left us a witness in His Word. So how does God's Word address our emotions and questions when we face loss and doubt? God is able to secure the promises delivered to Isaiah and to us because of who He is. To better understand what God does, we first need to consider who God is. At this point we need to introduce a theological idea that will be considered over and over again throughout this study—providence.

Like God's name in the Book of Esther, the word *providence* never appears in Scripture. However, this doctrine defines the way God works in the world. *Providence* refers to His invisible work in our lives—His unceasing involvement in the world. It's the belief that God stewards His creation in such a way that all creation ultimately fulfills His intended purpose.

Read Ephesians 1:11. What does this verse teach about God's intentionality and control of the world?

Read Romans 11:36. What attributes do we learn about God from this verse? How do these attributes relate to our lives?

One of God's chief attributes is His sovereignty. *Sovereignty* refers to His rule over all His creation. Absolutely nothing escapes His power and influence. God is in charge of all things because He has created and sustains all things. He's radically, utterly in control.

Often people struggle with the truth of God's sovereignty because it means we must relinquish ultimate control to Him. However, God's sovereignty should comfort us.

If you're being honest, what aspects of God's sovereignty make you uncomfortable?

Read Isaiah 46:9-10. List three comforts you can take as a believer in knowing that God is sovereign.

1.

2.

3.

Comfort comes in knowing that God is in control. Because God is sovereign, we can have peace when life's situations become confusing or chaotic. Another comfort lies in our increased ability to rest when worry or anxiety seeks to dominate our hearts and minds. Trusting in God's sovereignty removes fear from the equation, opening the door to greater joy and contentment. John Calvin wrote:

> *Ignorance of Providence is the greatest of all miseries,*
> *and the knowledge of it the highest happiness.*[1]

How could increasing your trust in God's ultimate control affect your emotions and outlook?

Read the following verse.

> The LORD has established His throne in the heavens,
> And His sovereignty rules over all.
> PSALM 103:19

How did the psalmist describe God's rule?

In what ways do you need to trust God's control and release your own?

You can rest in this one simple, repeated truth of Scripture: God rules over all. If you've spent large portions of your life worrying about details, anxious about every twist, turn, detour, or roadblock on your path, consider ways a greater understanding of and trust in God's sovereignty can change your life. Would you like to reduce your ongoing concerns and negative emotions? Applying yourself to the diligent study and application of God's sovereignty will do just that.

✶ PRAYER ✶

Ask God to give you insight into ways you can trust Him more and rest in His sovereign care. Ask Him to open your eyes to recognize His invisible hand along the pathway of your days.

---

1. John Calvin, *Institutes of the Christian Religion*, trans. Henry Beveridge, ed. Anthony Uyl (Ontario: Devoted, 2016), 1.17.11.

⊙ **DAY 2** ⊙

LETTING GO OF THE WHEEL

Sometimes it seems as if our culture is obsessed with control. We control the temperatures in our home, and now we can do that from our smartphones. We control our schedules through daily planners or apps. We even control our time with God, giving Him five minutes in the morning or fifteen minutes at lunch. We seek to control our health; environment; and even, at times, the people around us.

Our desire to keep things under control helps improve our lives and surroundings. But it can also hinder us from living in a spirit of surrender that a life under God's overarching control requires.

In recent months how have you sought to control circumstances in your life?

Do you follow a fixed schedule? How do you react if that schedule is interrupted?

Admittedly, not everyone feels the need to control all things at all times. Some people are more flexible than others. But within most of us is a desire to control at least the important areas of our lives, such as health, safety, and provision. This impulse stems from our need for security as human beings.

Read Luke 12:22-26. Summarize Jesus' words.

Do you think it's possible to follow Jesus' instructions in these verses at all times? Why or why not?

What does our worry about our circumstances communicate about our faith in God?

Worry is the greatest revealer of doubt. The ravens in Jesus' example own a simple faith that often eludes us. Consider when you purchase something online and you receive an email alerting you that your item will arrive the next day. Do you then spend time the remainder of that day worrying about whether your item will arrive? No. Why not? Because you've been assured that your order was received and filled. If you chose to worry about an order you placed, despite being told the exact delivery date of that item, you would reveal doubt not only in the company's ability to stay true to its word but also in its ability to provide the item you ordered.

More than we trust an online store to deliver a package in two days, we should trust God to sustain our lives. Not only does God rule over all, but He's also the owner of all. As He said through Jeremiah:

> Behold, I am the LORD, the God of all flesh;
> is anything too difficult for Me?
> JEREMIAH 32:27

Nothing is too difficult for God. When we choose to worry or inadvertently allow worry to enter our thoughts and actions, we're questioning His sovereign control. We're questioning His ability to stay true to His Word. We're questioning His ability to provide what He says He will provide.

Recall a time when you felt worried or anxious about a certain direction your life had taken, yet in hindsight you saw that God's hand had directed your circumstances all along. What did you learn through that experience?

Maybe you're saying, "But Tony, I never worry or doubt God." However, God declared through Jeremiah:

> The heart is deceitful above all things
> and beyond cure.
> JEREMIAH 17:9, NIV

If you feel that you never worry or doubt, take a moment to ask God to enlighten your heart to recognize hidden areas of doubt and anxiety in which you may need to trust His sovereignty.

Whether our worry levels are high or low, we can grow in our level of faith in God. We start growing when we understand God's providence and sovereignty. Yesterday we defined *sovereignty* as God's rule over all His creation. *Providence* refers to God's control of the spinning wheel of history behind the scenes.

Providence is actually a subcategory of sovereignty. In other words, one way God exercises His sovereignty is by His providence. The providence of God is the miraculous, mysterious way He intersects and interconnects events in order to bring about His sovereign rule of the universe. God's sovereignty is what He wants to happen. God's providence is the way He orders and connects events to bring about His will.

As humans, we often misunderstand God's providence. To achieve His ultimate sovereign purposes, God at times providentially allows things to take place that are outside His preferences. In His sovereignty God allows things He doesn't prefer in order to accomplish His ultimate plan.

> **Think about all that's involved in baking a cake. What would it taste like if you chose to eat the ingredients separately rather than as a completed, baked cake?**

> **How is a fully baked caked different from the separate ingredients?**

When we see our circumstances outside God's providence and sovereignty, we aren't seeing our lives the way God intended. It would be like taking a recipe for cake and eating the separate ingredients before baking them together. However, when we see our circumstance through God's providence and sovereignty, we see the ingredients coming together to produce something beautiful.

Read Esther 2:1-17. Then answer the following questions.

Based on what we've learned about God's providence and sovereignty, how should we understand Esther's ascent to royalty?

Why would God tell this story without using His name? In what ways do you see Him at work?

We don't read God's name in Esther 2, but He's there. Esther became the queen through the providential work of God. Without an understanding of providence and sovereignty, these events may seem like luck or fate. This seeming twist of fate would have far-reaching consequences for God's people. Only when we understand the link between providence and sovereignty can we recognize God's fingerprints in the midst of His apparent absence. We don't always get to see how God weaves the details of our lives to take us to our intended destination and purpose. He operates behind the scenes, pulling the strings and setting the stage. His ways are always designed to produce the greatest outcome for His purposes and for our spiritual development.

When seeking to trace God's sovereign purpose, we're usually shortsighted. Neglecting to look beyond our immediate situation, relationship, job, or challenge, we easily become confused. Things may not (and probably don't) make sense when viewed individually rather than as part of an entire tapestry of scenarios God weaves together to accomplish His overarching plan.

✳ PRAYER ✳

Pray that the Holy Spirit will enable you to view your life
through spiritual eyes that allow you not only to trust what
you can't see but also to identify patterns in God's sovereign
plan as His invisible hand weaves the pieces together.

⊙ DAY 3 ⊙

HOW GOD DRIVES

Take a moment to think about your car. Consider all of the different parts and pieces that fit together to form your car. Some cars have small trunks, while others have large trunks. Some cars sit close to the ground, while others can nearly triple that height. Some cars go fast. Others seem built to glide along at a leisurely pace.

Cars are different in many ways. But they're also alike in many ways. Does your car have a steering wheel? Tires? How about a seat for you to sit in? I've seen a lot of cars over the course of my life, and they come in all shapes and sizes, but these features remain consistent in all of them: they all have steering wheels, tires, and seats.

The pathways we travel along to reach God's destiny for our lives won't be identical. Some of us will get there faster than others. Some may have to carry a lot of baggage with them. Some may arrive there comfortably, while some may have a bumpy ride. Yet despite the many differences we'll encounter on the various pathways of our spiritual journeys, we'll all share certain similarities.

For example, followers of Jesus Christ all share the reality that God works all things together for good to those who love Him and are called for His purpose (see Rom. 8:28). No matter how difficult the journey, no matter how challenging the trip, and no matter how precarious the pathway, providence means God caused it for a greater purpose. This truth applies to each of us, even though our journeys to our destinies may come in all shapes and sizes.

Read Romans 8:28-29. Why does God cause all things to work together for good?

Now read Ephesians 1:12-14. What's another reason God causes all things to work together for good?

All things work together according to God's agency—His determined providential involvement. Not only does God cause all things to work together for good so that we'll be "conformed to the image of His Son" (Rom. 8:29), but He also does it with the intended outcome being "to the praise of His glory" (Eph. 1:12,14). Work works all things for good to conform us to the likeness of Jesus and to exalt His name. His providence guarantees that all He has created fulfills and satisfies its created purpose, which is to bring glory to Himself.

God exists for God. So does everything He made. He made it all for Himself. That's the reason it's here. That's the reason we're here. We're made for God. Our lives aren't about us; they're about Him and His glory. If you don't care for that idea, go and make your own universe. God made this one, so He gets to set the rules.

Anything that competes with, negates, or minimizes God's glory exists in a perpetual state of misalignment (see Rom. 1:18-32). It's out of order. God made all things to display His attributes, character, and power (see Col. 1:15-17; Rev. 4:11).

Read Colossians 1:17. What does it mean for God to hold "all things" together?

In what ways does God receive glory through the events and circumstances in our lives? How might we get in the way of God's work in our lives?

Everything you and I possess has been given to us as a direct result of God's choice to do so. Everything you've received was created either by God or from materials He created. God produces every single thing. Because He does, He claims sovereignty over it all as well. He controls it. He's intricately, intimately involved in every single detail of life. If He stepped back for a moment and didn't hold the universe in place, everything would descend into chaos. We'd all be obliterated in an instant.

From God's vantage point, it all makes perfect sense. Yet from ours, time can seem marked by an endless array or series of contingencies we may call bad luck, chance, or random events. That may be the way it seems, but it's not how it is. Nothing is random with God. Consider God's foresight and knowledge in contrast to your own:

> I *am God, and there is no other;*
> I *am God, and there is no one like Me,*
> *Declaring the end from the beginning,*
> *And from ancient times things which have not been done,*
> *Saying, "My purpose will be established,*
> *And I will accomplish all My good pleasure";*
> *Calling a bird of prey from the east,*
> *The man of My purpose from a far country.*
> *Truly I have spoken; truly I will bring it to pass.*
> I *have planned it, surely I will do it.*
> ISAIAH 46:9-11

One problem in remaining on the right path as we head toward our purpose is that we don't see the end as God does. And when we can't see where we're headed, we get frustrated and feel lost. Have you ever felt frustrated when you were driving and got lost? Yet when you found a map or a GPS or got directions from a stranger, your frustration dissipated. Why? Because reaching your destination came into sight.

While we may be directionally challenge, God isn't. He has perfect knowledge of our destination. Unlike us, He can see the end from the beginning. However, along the pathways of His providential leading, He doesn't always give us the directions to the very end. He doesn't provide us with the full map view so that we can see every turn we'll eventually take. He gives us a glimpse here, a direction there, or the next step but rarely the entire picture. Thus, people often live in a perpetual state of frustration, not knowing how each step, each day, each set of circumstances, or each conversation is leading to the right place. Without a full view of providence and a surrender to sovereignty, these frustrations can overflow in an overwhelming cascade of emotions.

Describe how you feel when you're lost. How do your emotions change after you locate the right directions or get on the right road to where you're going?

What might God be teaching us by not taking us on a direct route but instead on one with twists, turns, and detours?

What reasons has God given you to trust Him even when the path isn't clear? Spend a few moments meditating on God's faithfulness to you.

Nothing comes to you that doesn't first pass through God's providential fingers. You have to believe that. You have to trust that. You have to rest in that. That mindset will position you to respond to life's challenges, setbacks, and seemingly random occurrences with a spirit of intentionality and persevering faith.

Believing that God is working all things for our good and His glory means we continually choose to place our trust in Him, recognizing that all the twists and turns along the path are producing His image in us (see Rom. 8:29). Not only that, but every hardship is preparing for you "an eternal weight of glory far beyond all comparison" (2 Cor. 4:17).

✴ PRAYER ✴

As you pray throughout the day, engage God in a conversation about His direction for your life. Ask for a deep, abiding trust in Jesus. Ask for greater grace to trust God along the pathway of your life so that you can be set free from worry and so that your faith in God can be built up.

PULL OVER AND TAKE A BREAK

Every January at the church I pastor we hold a solemn assembly, a dedicated week when we come together as a congregation to fast, pray, and commit our lives and our year to the Lord. We don't dictate rules for fasting. We simply ask that with God's guidance, members choose something from which to fast for one week.

Some members fast from food, a meal, or even chocolate. Other members give up watching television, while some give up social media. Fasting is letting go of something in the physical realm in order to focus on something in the spiritual realm. I've heard countless testimonies of how fasting during the solemn assembly at church ushered in life transformations, rescued marriages, and resurrected hope.

It recently struck me that it might be beneficial if each of us chose to fast from something intangible as well. That could be fasting from worry, letting go of control, rejecting critical thoughts, or giving up doubt. Each time this desire or impulse sought to spark its light in our minds, we simply reminded ourselves, *I'm fasting from worry right now, so I can't indulge that thought.*

Essentially, that's what discovering how to trust in God's providential care can do for us. The more we trust His providence, the more we learn to let go of preoccupations like worry, critical thoughts, doubt, and a need for control.

List three events or circumstances that can prompt you to worry, fear, or doubt.

1.

2.

3.

Read John 15:5. Jesus clearly said apart from Him we can do nothing. In what ways should this truth affect you and your emotions?

How can a spiritual discipline like fasting teach us that we're not in control?

People rarely like providence. People like to be in control. It's true. Only when providence is ushering us toward a seen result with visible rewards do we embrace providence. Why? Because people prefer autonomy, and autonomy precludes God's rule. We don't like to let go. Fasting is good for our souls because fasting leads us to feel our helplessness in a way that points us toward God. It allows us to rest in God's control and release our grip on the circumstances of our lives.

When we understand and accept God's providence, we lay down our own paths, our own pursuits, and our own maneuverings to try getting to where we feel we need to go. Trusting in God's providence requires letting go. Providence lifts our hand. Providence acknowledges that ultimately God is in control and that His method of being in control often involves twists, turns, and meanderings that make us uncomfortable.

Yet the sovereign providence of God can only mean that He's the absolute ruler, controller, and sustainer of all aspects of His creation. He's the sovereign King. He's running the universe. His prowess and wisdom set up details; turn circumstances; reverse situations; and usher people, positions, and places into His intended purpose. Often all this occurs without our awareness or acceptance because God doesn't need us as much as we may think He does.

Though God doesn't ultimately need us, He uses us to accomplish His purposes. What joy should we find in being used by God?

When has God used you despite your limitations or perhaps even your unwillingness to be used by Him?

In hindsight how did these occurrences affirm God's providence in your life?

God's Word features accounts of His will and purpose succeeding despite human weakness. In His providence God spoke through a donkey (see Num. 22:21-31). He also woke up a king in order to position Esther to save His people from anni-hilation (see Esth. 6:1).In His providence He used tired, hungry foot soldiers and priests to march around a wall and produce one of the most amazing military feats of all time (see Josh. 6:1-20). God's providence and sovereign control exist, whether or not we acknowledge them. Thus, to discover the importance of working, living, and moving within them is one of the most critical life skills we could ever develop.

Unfortunately, this wisdom is often lost on our egos. Why? Because most people want to do what they want to do. Most people want to feel as if they're calling the shots. Most people want to be the center attraction in the three-ring circus known as their lives. So they deny or rebel against the truth of sovereignty in their hearts and their minds. Yet denying or rebelling against God's providence doesn't make it less true. It just makes us feel that we have more control than we actually do. In fact, rebellion against God is typically rooted in a desire to usurp His sovereignty. Furthermore, God can even use people's rebellion to accomplish His plan.

Read Exodus 9:34-35 and Romans 9:14-18. What do these verses say about God's ability to use a human being's rebellion for His ultimate goal?

How can God use something meant for evil to ultimately accomplish good? What are some biblical examples when God used an evil intention to bring about good?

How does knowing that God can bring good from evil circumstances make you feel about a challenge you're facing?

If you've spent time wandering the pathway of life, wondering why bad things happen to good people or how God can allow certain circumstances in your life, these truths are for you right now. As you discover the security of sovereignty, you'll experience the peace that's rightfully yours as a child of the King.

The greatest truth you can ever know about God, other than hearing and receiving the message of salvation, is His sovereignty. When you know God is in control—even of things that appear to be out of control—you're able to move through life benefiting from the blessings of assurance, peace, and contentment. When you truly understand that He's in your corner as your greatest defender and vindicator, you'll no longer seek to rescue yourself. Only in drawing close to Him so that you can hear Him and, as a result, follow Him can you experience His deliverance in every area of your life.

✳ PRAYER ✳

Prioritize time to think about God's control and
ultimate power over all. Consider ways He has
worked in other people's lives or in your own life
to bring good results or positive growth from a
negative situation. Thank Him for His ability and
care to do that in His gracious sovereign purpose.

LOST IN LOGIC

When we face a trial or an adverse situation in life, we often try to figure it out, fix it, or logically argue our way through it.

When has God done anything in your life that seemed illogical at the time but turned out to be something great? If this hasn't happened to you, when have you seen this happen to someone else?

What do you notice about the various paths by which God led His people when delivering them throughout the Bible?

What do you notice about God as He delivered His people?

When we rely too much on our logic and reasoning, we leave ourselves vulnerable to the outcome of that reasoning instead of preparing ourselves for God's intervention. God is in control. I don't care how things appear to you right now. I don't care what authority your boss has over you right now. I don't care what your addiction, your mate, or your messy situation is telling you to do. None of those people or circumstances are in ultimate control.

Yes, they may look as though they are. After all, during the exodus Pharaoh had every appearance of control over the Israelites as his army chased them across the wilderness and backed them up against an enormous body of water (see Ex. 14:5-31). But what we see is never all there is to be seen. Sovereignty can reshape water and set souls free. Providence can pave a way where there seems to be no way at all. God is in control.

In what ways can human logic get in the way of identifying and following God's direction?

What might we miss if God worked only in ways that made sense to us?

Consider the example Paul gave the Corinthians:

> *Since in the wisdom of God the world through its wisdom did not come to know God, God was well-pleased through the foolishness of the message preached to save those who believe. For indeed Jews ask for signs and Greeks search for wisdom; but we preach Christ crucified, to Jews a stumbling block and to Gentiles foolishness, but to those who are the called, both Jews and Greeks, Christ the power of God and the wisdom of God. Because the foolishness of God is wiser than men, and the weakness of God is stronger than men.*
> 1 CORINTHIANS 1:21-25

Why would Jesus' crucifixion seem like foolishness from a human perspective?

How did Paul address the argument that the cross was foolish?

We look back at the cross with the benefit of time, but for the first-century audience, the cross didn't make sense. For the Jews, being crucified meant being cursed and forsaken by God. To them, Jesus' death was a sign that He wasn't who He claimed to be. To the Greeks, crucifixion was a mark of shame. It would have been unbelievable to them. Worshiping a crucified criminal would have been nonsense.

However, the cross is foolish only from a human perspective. Despite its folly the cross demonstrated the wisdom and power of God. As Peter pointed out, Jesus was "delivered over by the predetermined plan and foreknowledge of God" (Acts 2:23). In other words, what might seem illogical to the world was the perfect plan of God. The Father allowed human evil against His Son to fulfill His purpose.

God has a myriad of reasons for what He does and for what He allows:

> "My thoughts are not your thoughts,
>   Nor are your ways My ways," declares the LORD.
> "For as the heavens are higher than the earth,
>   So are My ways higher than your ways
>   And My thoughts than your thoughts."
> ISAIAH 55:8-9

God's vantage point is so far above our own that when we seek to interject our logic or rationale into the equation, it's like trying to put together a puzzle with only a fraction of the pieces. Logically figuring out God's ways will never happen, simply because we don't have all the information.

Sometimes God delays us on our pathway because He's seeking to develop our character or our passion for something He wants us to do. Sometimes He delays because He's seeking to develop a quality within someone else with whom we'll come in contact later. Or at times He's ordering events so that their timing intersects with the plan He wants to carry out. Always keep in mind that He's the great, unfiguroutable God. He doesn't always disclose His purposes until we're much further along our pathway.

Read the following verses.

> We also exult in our tribulations, knowing that tribulation
> brings about perseverance; and perseverance, proven character;
> and proven character, hope; and hope does not disappoint,
> because the love of God has been poured out within our
> hearts through the Holy Spirit who was given to us.
> ROMANS 5:3-5

> The testing of your faith produces endurance.
> JAMES 1:3

**What are some reasons God allows difficulties, challenges, and roadblocks
along the pathways of our lives?**

Whenever God sovereignly allows something that's unpleasant, always remember
that it's also not random. He allowed it for a reason. God always has a reason for
what He does and for what He allows. The Book of Lamentations tells us:

> If He causes grief,
> Then He will have compassion
> According to His abundant lovingkindness.
> LAMENTATIONS 3:32

**Do you find it easy or difficult to trust God when circumstances don't
make logical sense? Explain.**

**If you're facing a difficult situation or a roadblock, what would it look like
to let go of your need to devise an outcome and surrender to God instead?**

Of the Scriptures we've considered this week, which ones have stuck with you? Which are most helpful to you in confronting the roadblocks you're currently facing?

It's difficult to trust God if you don't believe He's sovereign. When things happen in your life that are painful or confusing and you don't fully grasp God's sovereignty, it's easy to lose trust in God's control and goodness. But once you grab and hold on to the truth that He's the ruler, controller, sustainer, and authority over all, the seemingly disconnected happenings of life are woven together into a tapestry of His perfect timing. The meanderings that seem to take you from place to place on the pathway of your days now lead somewhere. And although you may not see the destination or be instantly relieved of the difficulties, your trust in God's providential care and sovereign rule will give you the ability to rest rather than fret, be still rather than be anxious, and praise rather than complain.

I hope this week's study has helped you realize more about God's sovereign and providential character. These two essentially beliefs about God are the backbone of the Book of Esther and this Bible study. When you understand the sovereignty of God even though you don't understand what He's doing, you'll learn how to see God in a way you've never seen Him before. You'll find joy in His providence. You'll discover the power of His presence and the purpose of His plans.

✳ PRAYER ✳

Read Romans 8:28-29 and focus on this passage today
as often as you can. Seek to align your mind with God's
sovereignty by letting go of your logic and trusting
in His divine direction. Ask God to increase your faith
so that you can rest more fully in His providential care.

Week 2

MILE MARKERS

Start

Welcome to group session 2 of Pathways.

Imagine a trip you frequently take (from work to home, to the gym, etc.) What's a mile marker that lets you know you've almost reached your destination?

What's an example of a spiritual mile marker on your journey with God?

Before we begin, read aloud Esther 3:1–4:8 together as a group. The passage is summarized below.

The incident in these chapters took place about five years after the installation of Queen Esther (see 2:16; 3:7). Haman is identified as an Agagite, perhaps a descendant of the Amalekite king Agag, who was defeated but spared by King Saul (see 1 Sam. 15). Israel and Amalek were enemies from the time of Moses (see Ex. 17:8-16).

Although other people bowed to Haman, Mordecai refused to worship him because of his Jewish faith, just as Daniel had declined to worship King Darius (see Dan. 6). Haman masterminded a plot to exterminate all of the Jews. The divinely appointed day and month were determined by casting lots. When Mordecai learned about the murderous plot, he and all of the Jews joined in mourning, fasting, and wearing sackcloth and ashes. Esther learned about the decree from her messenger, who relayed Mordecai's plea for her help.

Watch

Complete this viewer guide as you watch video session 2.

Mile markers are signs that God gives us along the way that His providence is steering us to His divine kingdom purpose and destination for our lives.

Mile marker 1: spiritual warfare

Spiritual warfare is where there is an attack by the evil one, through his surrogates, in order to keep God's kingdom from expanding and keep His promises from being fulfilled.

The Book of Esther is about a spiritual battle that seeks to thwart the kingdom of God and negate the promises of God.

God's purpose was a promise that He made to His people. His purpose is a promise that He makes to you and me.

In trials God wants to use you and what you're going through to further His kingdom.

Mile marker 2: opportunities

God has called us to represent Him on earth and to intersect for the kingdom of heaven against the onslaught of the kingdom of hell.

God wants you to be a channel of blessing. He doesn't want you to be a cul de sac; He wants you to be a conduit.

Mile marker 3: a faith risk

Faith involves acting like it is so even when it's not so in order that it might be so, simply because God said so.

Video sessions available at lifeway.com/pathways or with a subscription to smallgroup.com

Discuss

Discuss the video with your group, using the following questions.

Look back through Esther 3:1–4:8. Where do we see the three mile markers spiritual warfare, opportunities, and a faith risk in this passage of Esther?

Dr. Evans taught that the first mile marker is spiritual warfare. Read Ephesians 6:12. What is spiritual warfare? When should we expect to encounter it?

Read Matthew 4:1-11. How did Jesus respond to spiritual warfare? What does His response teach us about the way we should prepare for and fight spiritual battles?

The second mile marker is taking advantage of our opportunities. Are you currently in a cul de sac or a conduit? How are you using the ways God has blessed you to serve others?

What opportunities exist for this group as a whole to use what God is doing in your lives? What ministry could you engage in or pursue together?

The third mile marker is a faith risk. Read Hebrews 11:1. When was the last time you took a step of faith?

In the video Dr. Evans said, "If all you see is what you see, you do not see all there is to be seen." How does faith help us see beyond what's right in front of us?

When Haman asked Esther to implore the king's favor (see Esth. 4:8), he was asking her to take a substantial risk. Why should we seek to be faithful to God despite the risks?

How should we deal with the fear of the unknown that comes from taking a risk?

Read week 2 and complete the activities before the next group session.

Mile Markers

D. L. Moody wrote these words in his Bible beside Isaiah 6:8. They say, "I am only one, but I am one. I cannot do everything, but I can do something. And that which I can do, by the grace of God, I will do."[1]

Studying Queen Esther or other biblical characters can sometimes cause us to stall rather than move forward in our lives. Why? Because these people often loom larger than life in our collective imaginations. We forget they were human and had to make daily choices that led to their great impact. Some of these choices were monumental, as when Esther entered the king's chambers unannounced. Others were seemingly insignificant, as when she followed the eunuch's advice on what to take with her when she saw the king for the first time. Whether large or small, choices combine to craft the entirety of a hero's story.

Yet in our contemporary culture, which largely focuses on entertainment, movies, and competitions on a grand scale, we can sometimes lessen the value we place on everyday obedience to God in the smallest details. We want to be the hero. Save the day. Or even save the planet.

But reaching your destination—your destiny—on the pathway where God has placed you requires a step-by-step process. It demands faithfulness along the journey. It summons steadfastness even in times that may seem inconsequential or trivial. Heroes are heroes because they made wise choices, even when those choices seemed small. They were consistently obedient to God.

In this week's lesson we'll look at ways we can know we're on the right path. These mile markers tell us we're headed in the right direction and enable us to keep going even when nothing incredible seems to be taking place. The ever-influential D. L. Moody recognized his limitations in acknowledging that he could do only what he could do. But it was this level of wisdom that enabled him to do all that he, as one man, could do. History would prove that what he did was more than most.

Never belittle the solitary steps or the long, seemingly endless journey on the pathway to which God has called you. When you're faithful in little, He will cause the little things to add up to be much in His kingdom.

1. D. L. Moody, GraceQuotes.com, accessed October 4, 2018, https://gracequotes.com/category/dl-moody/.

> **This week's teaching draws out themes found in Esther 3:1–4:8.**
> **Review this passage of Scripture before beginning your personal study.**

⊙ **DAY 1** ⊙

HITTING THE ROAD

Have you ever taken a road trip that seemed to stretch on forever? If you've ever driven in west Texas or someplace similar, it can seem that the same patch of road and terrain repeats itself again and again. Even though an hour or more has gone by, it may appear that you've gotten nowhere at all.

That's where mile markers come in. Mile markers tell you what point of the pathway you're on. Every highway or interstate in America provides these mile markers—small signs designating the particular mile where you are. They conveniently show you how far you've traveled and allow you to count down the distance to an upcoming exit.

Similarly, God has set mile markers in our lives as we travel the pathway to our destinies. If and when we learn how to identify them, we'll gain insight into how far we've come and how much farther we have to go.

What are some mile markers God has given you to let you know where you are on the path toward your destiny?

What are some indicators of your personal calling or purpose that God has revealed to you?

Have you experienced any development in your sense of calling through the years? In what ways?

Esther was raised to the position of queen and was then asked to step out in faith. God placed Esther as queen not only for her benefit but also for the preservation of His chosen people. However, in taking this step of faith, Esther risked everything. Like Esther, you weren't placed in the position you're in just for yourself. You weren't given your skills, talents, connections, and personality for your benefit alone. When you look back over the course of your life, you start to see a pattern of preparation as God has equipped you for the destination where He's taking you. This pattern of preparation is leading you toward your calling or purpose.

Your calling involves a combination of many factors, such as your talents, interests, background, experience, passion, personality, and connections. When all of these elements merge at the same point on life's path, God is placing you in a position to fulfill your purpose. Identifying some of the pieces that make up your purpose can help clarify the direction God wants to take you in life.

List three of your talents or skills. You can keep them vague, such as interpersonal relationships, organizing information, and so on.

1.

2.

3.

List three areas of interest to you. Examples might be reading, athletics, and cultural awareness.

1.

2.

3.

Identify one pursuit you're passionate about.

Finally, list three aspects of your personality, such as introverted, talkative, deliberative, or spontaneous.

1.

2.

3.

None of the qualities and interests you listed are random. God gave you each one for His intended purpose, just as He did for Esther. Her history, heart, and humanity combined to align her life with the perfect divine purpose of delivering her people from certain death.

- Esther's background as an orphan no doubt gave her compassion for the downtrodden and a sympathetic connection to people in need.
- Esther's heart for her uncle and the Jews emboldened her to carry out her destiny by going before the king to request intervention on their behalf.
- Esther's humanity—her personality and beauty—provided the opportunity for her to intervene for her people, because these traits played a major role in enabling her to be chosen as queen.

Similarly, God has a plan for you. A plan that will bring Him glory and others good. A plan that will involve the unique combination of your own history, heart, and humanity as well.

Review Esther 3:1–4:8, considering why God might have raised up Esther to be queen at the same time Haman was plotting against the Jews.

How do we see God intentionally working behind these scenes in this story?

At the same time Esther was being raised to be the queen of Persia, another royal official, Haman, was plotting to destroy the Jews because of his hatred of Mordecai. It's no coincidence that these events happened at the same time. God used Esther's gifts and position at the perfect time so that He could redeem His people through her faithfulness. Esther served her purpose. All faithfulness requires is that you serve your God-ordained purpose.

What happens when we compare our purpose and calling in the kingdom with someone else's purpose and calling?

Far too often we fall prey to the illusion that our lives don't matter or that we don't have a specific purpose on earth. We can blame this tendency on many causes, but one of the prominent ones is comparison. The increase in using social media has led to an increase in personal comparisons, which in turn have led to a drought of personal self-worth. Couple this trend with our culture's worship of celebrities, and a number of people just can't seem to find contentment in or even an awareness of their purpose in life. God's purpose for you isn't the same as His purpose for the people you follow on social media or for the celebrities you see on TV.

Though your purpose may not seem as significant as Esther's, it's just as important, just as critical, and just as valuable. When you're driving, you sometimes hear the phrase "Eyes on the road." Similarly, when you're pursuing your purpose on the pathway God has placed you on, keep your eyes on His mile markers in your life, not on other people. Look at the ways He's positioning you for such a time as this.

✷ PRAYER ✷

Loving Heavenly Father, give me the heart, insight, and
perspective to view my purpose through Your eyes. Help me
not to ignore the gifts, talents, and desires You've placed in
me. Give me patience while You arrange the prerequisites
and details for fully living out Your calling for me.
I trust You along the pathway. In Christ's name, amen.

YOUR PURPOSE IS BEYOND YOU

A friend was driving through Dallas when he rounded a curve on a fairly busy tollway, only to discover a ladder lying in the middle of the road, apparently having fallen off a truck. He quickly swerved to miss it and then called to inform the authorities so that they could remove the ladder. Thankfully, no one was hurt. A ladder in the middle of a busy tollway could prove disastrous.

The same thing is true of ladders that are leaning against the wrong wall. The disaster might not be as graphic or immediately noticeable, but the impact could be just as tragic. It's nothing short of a disaster for someone to spend the bulk of their time, energy, and emotions pursuing a goal or a purpose, only to discover it wasn't the correct goal or purpose.

Yet that's the case for many people today. In fact, many Christians will have spent a large part of their lives climbing the ladder of success, only to discover at the end that it was leaning against the wrong wall. In an effort to meet the standards of our world's system and our world's idea of success, many people will have missed the purposes of God. They may be accomplished in their education, careers, and wealth, but they'll stand before God never having finished the work He had created them to do.

One reason we aren't raptured at the moment of conversion is that God leaves us here to accomplish His kingdom purpose.

Have you experienced a season in your life when the goal or purpose you were seeking proved futile or unimportant? Describe the way this misplaced effort affected you and those around you.

It's easy to get off the right path and pursue goals that don't lie within God's purpose for us. Examples include the pursuit of people, possessions, paychecks, power, popularity, and perhaps even some piety sprinkled in there to make us feel better.

Yet when our pursuits aren't tied to the kingdom and God's overarching agenda, we've missed the mark of His purpose for our lives.

> **Review Esther 2:8-20. What tangible blessings might Esther have experienced by being named the queen of Persia?**

> **In what ways could these blessings have led to complacency and prevented Esther from taking a risk to help her people?**

Esther embraced her preparation to become queen. Because she pleased Hegai, the king's eunuch, she received a better diet and care (see v. 9). She went through an extravagant yearlong beautification process (see v. 12). The king loved Esther more than all the other women and rewarded her according to the pleasure he took in her (see vv. 17-18). Esther lacked nothing. It would have been easy for her to enjoy these benefits and coast into a life of comfort and opulence. Later in the story God would call her to risk all of this for the sake of her God and her people. Later we'll see what this risk involved.

God's purposes often come coupled with sacrifice. This is why Scripture often emphasizes qualities like courage and faith.

> **Read Joshua 1:6-9 and highlight every reference to courage or a lack of fear.**

God gave these instructions to a leader and military commander. We might assume a military commander, of all people, wouldn't have to be told to have courage. But knowing Joshua's heart and the difficult task that lay ahead, God emphasized this quality time and time again. If Joshua had to be reminded to have courage, imagine how much more courage a young, unexperienced woman like Esther would have needed. Each of us needs to remember that pursuing the pathway of God's purpose for our lives will require courage.

Describe a time in your life when God led you to do something or say something that required courage or faith.

Why do you think God calls us to do things that require courage and faith?

Pursuing God's purpose often requires taking courageous steps of faith. Before we go any further, I want you to examine your personal views of courage and faith.

Read the following verses.

> When I am afraid,
> I will put my trust in You.
> In God, whose word I praise,
> In God I have put my trust;
> I shall not be afraid.
> What can mere man do to me?
> PSALM 56:3-4

> You have not received a spirit of slavery leading
> to fear again, but you have received a spirit of adoption
> as sons by which we cry out, "Abba! Father!"
> ROMANS 8:15

> God has not given us a spirit of timidity,
> but of power and love and discipline.
> 2 TIMOTHY 1:7

Based on these verses, where does fear come from?

These verses make clear that fear is a given fact of life. They don't tell us to avoid, ignore, or deny it. Instead, how should we address our fear?

How would you express the strategy these verses provide for living with courage?

One way you'll know you're on the path to God's purpose for your life is that you'll be required to place your trust in God in order to take the next step on the path to your destiny. God often asks us to do things that are beyond our own abilities and comfort so that we'll have the opportunity to see Him work. That way He receives all the glory when we carry out His purpose.

Until we're willing to press forward in spite of our fears and discomfort, we'll find ourselves stuck at the roadblock called resistance.

Where do you need to press forward in your purpose despite fear and obstacles?

Who's a wise friend you could look to for support as you press forward on your pathway to purpose?

✳ PRAYER ✳

Loving Christ, teach me how to place my trust in You to such a degree that I'm willing to take risks in following You. Show me the value of great faith on the pathway to my destiny. Help me not to miss Your purpose for my life because of my comforts or security. In Your name, amen.

⊙ DAY 3 ⊙

PASSING THE TEST

If you'll remember your high-school or college days, you'll recall that you couldn't take some courses until certain other courses had been completed first. The courses that had to be taken first were called prerequisites. The educational institution had determined that certain fundamental information had to be mastered before the student could enroll in the next course. For example, before enrolling in algebra 2, a student must have taken and passed algebra 1. If foundational formulas weren't learned in algebra 1, it would be impossible to take and pass algebra 2.

Your pathway toward your purpose also has prerequisites. One of these prerequisites, which you studied yesterday, is learning how to trust God in the face of fear. Another prerequisite is passing the test of faith in spite of what you can or can't see. This test of faith might include taking a risk as you step out in obedience to what God has asked you to do.

Esther is a book about risk. Chapter 3 details Haman's plot against the Jews. In chapter 4 we see Esther and her cousin Mordecai begin to respond to the challenge of Haman's plot. Yet another prerequisite, as we discover in the life of Esther, is knowing what to do when we confront a dilemma we don't know how to tackle on our own.

> **Read James 1:5. When you face a difficult decision, why is it important to draw on the wisdom available to you?**

> **Read Jeremiah 33:3. Describe a time when God gave you insight or direction when you needed it and asked Him for it.**

Read Psalm 32:8. What three things did God say He will do for you? How have you experienced His doing any of these in your life?

1.

2.

3.

God gives us guidance, wisdom, insight, and direction in times when we face a decision or a dilemma and don't know what to do. We just need to seek Him, ask Him, and learn to listen to Him as He leads us. Often the times when we face a dilemma we don't know how to solve are exactly when God is arranging circumstances so that we can live out a specific purpose He's called us to. Typically, these are times of trial and testing.

God usually doesn't call us to fulfill a purpose during times when blessings rain down and life is going well. In fact, a person's purpose is often preceded by a deluge of testing. Passing these prerequisites, otherwise known as tests, moves you further along in your purpose. When your usefulness to the kingdom matches your calling, you're ready to fulfill the purpose God has for you.

Read Exodus 14:10-22. Briefly describe what happened and how the Israelites responded.

What dilemma did Moses face?

What test did Moses have to pass? In what way did God move Moses further on the pathway of his purpose when he passed the test?

When has God allowed you to be in a dilemma? What test did you need to pass? Describe what you learned from the experience.

People face many types of tests, often just before a breakthrough is about to occur. It could be a test of patience, as in the case of Joshua and Caleb, who had the courage to enter the promised land but had to wait forty years due to their fellow Israelites' lack of faith. It might be a test of obedience, as when God asked Abraham to sacrifice his son, Isaac, in whom he was placing the promise of his legacy. Or it might be a test of courage, as in the case of Esther.

Part of what it means to be a disciple and to be affirmed in your calling is to submit to learning, preparation, and testing. Whatever the test may be, you can be sure of this: if you don't pass it, there will be a retest, just like in school. God wants to make certain you pass the prerequisites necessary for fulfilling your purpose because within those prerequisites are the foundational principles and qualities you'll need to fully live out your destiny. Nothing could be worse than arriving at your destiny unable to live it out due to your lack of spiritual, emotional, or character development.

Read Ephesians 2:10 and Philippians 2:13. What's God's role in preparing us, motivating us, and carrying out our purpose?

Why do you think we try to rush ahead of our preparation for our purpose?

What are some dangers of arriving at a specific purpose or calling before we're adequately prepared?

Read the following verses.

*Consider it all joy, my brethren, when you encounter various
trials, knowing that the testing of your faith produces
endurance. And let endurance have its perfect result, so
that you may be perfect and complete, lacking in nothing.*
JAMES 1:2-4

Why should trials be met with joy?

**What's the fruit of going through trials? What would we miss if we were
never tested?**

Trials produce mature faith. In His great love for us, God patiently waits until
we're mature enough to live out our destinies before He ushers us into them. A
five-year-old wouldn't have a chance of passing a physics exam, so enrolling him
or her in a physics class would be cruel. God reveals His kindness to us in allowing
delays on the pathways we walk. He wants to be sure we pass the prerequisites
we'll need before we take the next step on the path to our purpose.

✳ PRAYER ✳

Lord and Savior, open my eyes to see ways You're testing me so that
I can seek Your wisdom, guidance, and strength in the midst of
them. Help me not to run ahead of the preparation and development
You're accomplishing in me. I want to be ready to do all You ask
me to do as I take each step on the path to Your purpose for me.

⊙ DAY 4 ⊙

TO BOW OR NOT TO BOW

The backstory of Esther's courage started with a man named Haman. A few years into her reign as queen, the king promoted Haman and gave him greater authority than anyone else at that time, other than himself. To recognize his new level of authority, all people were required to bow and pay homage to him.

As you might imagine, once the bowing had been decreed, the citizens of that region complied. That is, all but one man named Mordecai. Mordecai refused. Mordecai equated the act of bowing and paying homage with worship, and worshiping anyone other than God would be idolatry. Although he could respect Haman's role and position over him, he couldn't worship Haman. Mordecai reserved worship for God alone.

Read Esther 3:3-5. What were the results of Mordecai's refusal to bow?

Haman was incensed by Mordecai's dismissal of his personal esteem and honor. His refusal to bow filled Haman with so much hate that he determined to kill not only Mordecai but also all of Mordecai's people, the Jews.

Has God ever asked you to choose between honoring Him and honoring someone or something else? What was your decision, and what were the results?

Read Exodus 34:14. What's one reason we aren't to place anything in a higher position of honor than God?

Read 1 Samuel 15:2-3,9. When Saul failed to completely destroy the Amalekites, what conflict was set in motion for future generations of Israelities?

Because Haman was a descendant of the Amalekites, his hatred was fueled by more than a lack of honor shown by Mordecai. Haman's hatred came coupled with vengeance and reprisal, stirred on behalf of the blood of his ancestors. His thirst for power over the Jews didn't merely arise when his stature was elevated. It went decades deep into a history rife with racial conflict.

Mordecai's plot to rid his nation of the Jews was set in stone. The king had agreed, and now Esther and her people were on the pathway to total annihilation.

This circumstance brings us to another critical principle on how to discern whether it's your time to join God's purpose for your life. You know it's your time when God connects spiritual preparation with spiritual warfare.

Read Ephesians 6:12. What lies behind every conflict we face in the physical realm?

Why is it important to recognize the source of conflict as spiritual warfare?

Read Ephesians 6:13-18. What situation are you facing that could be brought to a conclusion by applying weapons of spiritual warfare?

According to 2 Corinthians 10:3-5, what do weapons of spiritual warfare have the power to accomplish?

Haman was an agent of the devil, whose goal was to thwart the purposes of God on earth. In the Old Testament this goal was carried out primarily through the targeting and destruction of the Jewish people, whom God declared that He would establish and protect and through whom the Messiah would come. Thus, throughout the history of the Jewish culture, we see a pattern of genocide and destruction. The Book of Esther dramatically portrays that effort.

In the New Testament, as well as in the age in which we live, Satan's destructive goal is directed at the church. Satan seeks to mute the effectiveness of the church, the men and women God has called to represent Him. To achieve this goal, he uses people and systems to seek to destroy God's program, promises, and purposes.

Whenever God is getting ready to use someone or a group of individuals, they'll have to fight battles. They'll have to face spiritual opposition. Satan's effort to destroy God's program and purpose includes you because you've been called to serve God. Your life isn't just about you. It's about God's greater plan, of which you're a part.

The aim of Haman's ploy to get rid of Mordecai wasn't just to get rid of Mordecai. It was a tool Satan used to incite and escalate rage in the heart of Haman so that he would set in motion a plan to obliterate an entire people from the planet. Spiritual battles occur on the pathways to purpose because an enemy is lurking on this same pathway, and he wants nothing more than to stop you in your tracks.

✶ PRAYER ✶

Dear Lord, open my eyes to recognize the source behind the challenges I face in my daily life. Help me wage warfare by using the tools You provide in Your Word. Let faith accompany me in every step I take so that I can reflect You and Your purposes for my life in all I do. In Christ's name, amen.

⊙ **DAY 5** ⊙

BLESSED TO BLESS

Spiritual warfare is a prerequisite for spiritual purpose. If you're not able to wage spiritual battle when Satan tries to thwart God's agenda, you're not ready to realize your ultimate spiritual destiny. Before God gives you spiritual responsibility, He wants to know that you have the wisdom and self-restraint to succeed against the schemes of the devil. He wants to know that you won't neglect your spiritual identity and resources when trouble comes.

When challenges come your way, it's easy to start relying on what you know to do in the natural realm. It's easy to leave the spiritual at bay when your path diverges into darkness. Yet it's only when you've demonstrated a reliance on spiritual weapons for spiritual battles that God will release you to fulfill your ultimate purpose.

Read the following verse.

> *Be of sober spirit, be on the alert. Your adversary, the devil,*
> *prowls around like a roaring lion, seeking someone to devour.*
> 1 PETER 5:8

How is the devil described in this verse? What does this description teach us about his nature?

How does being sober-minded help us stay alert to recognize spiritual warfare?

Spiritual warfare has a way of wearing down even the strongest among us. Consider what happened to Mordecai. The pain gets so deep, the desperation feels so great that hopelessness dominates our hearts and minds. This is exactly where Mordecai found himself when he heard that Haman's hatred extended beyond him to his people.

Read Esther 4:1. What was Mordecai's response to the news?

According to Esther 4:3, what did the Jewish people do in response to the news?

What can we learn from Mordecai's and the Jews' responses to the difficulty facing them?

God isn't opposed to the full expression of our emotions. Why do you think many of us try to hide our honest emotions from Him?

Keep in mind that while all this was taking place, Esther was living behind the walls of the palace. She hadn't heard of the destructive plan that Haman had set in place. In fact, she hadn't even spoken to the king in quite some time. But eventually, Esther found out about Mordecai's weeping and became deeply disturbed over what she heard. She then instructed one of her attendants to ask why Mordecai was so upset.

Read Esther 4:7-8. Describe Mordecai's response and his plan to solicit Esther's involvement.

Has someone ever sought your intervention in an urgent situation? How did you respond?

You know it's time for God to move you to your ultimate purpose when He places you in a position to leverage your influence for the advancement of His kingdom. This is exactly where Esther was. God hadn't providentially chosen her to be the queen simply because she was pretty. Rather, He used her beauty and temperament to position her for influence and impact. God knew the day would come when a military strategy against His chosen people would be instigated. He specifically positioned Esther for this situation.

When God has positioned you to leverage your influence for kingdom purposes and the advancement of His agenda for His people, you're securely on the pathway to your destiny. God always blesses you to be a blessing. He doesn't want the blessing to end with you but to flow through you.

Read Genesis 12:2. Why did God choose to bless Abram?

In what sense was the blessing Abram received supposed to extend beyond him? How did this promise play out in the remainder of Scripture?

Whenever you go to God to ask Him for a blessing, always keep in mind His purpose for blessing you. Always pray that He will use His blessings to you as blessings to others. Maintain that mindset as you go through each day, maximizing all God has given you in ways that will strengthen, bless, and help others. When God blesses you, He also has someone else in mind whom He wants you to bless.

As with Esther, God wants to know whether you'll use the pathway He has placed you on in ways that will advance His kingdom. Will you use the gifts, talents, skills, and resources He has given you to bring Him glory and expand His kingdom agenda on earth? Or will you simply use them for personal gain?

When you have little or no concern for God's kingdom in using the blessings He has given you, you've literally cut off your blessing. In fact, many people watch their blessings become curses when they choose to hoard them for personal gain rather than kingdom expansion. You're blessed to be a blessing. You're promoted to bring about promotion. You're equipped so that you can also equip. God intersects the circumstances and activities in our lives with those of other people in order to move His kingdom agenda forward.

Consider the ways God has blessed you. How are you using those blessings to bring good to others?

How can you increase the ways you're extending your blessings to others?

✶ PRAYER ✶

Loving Lord and Savior, help me recognize the blessings You've given to me and give me wisdom in using them to bless others. Forgive me for failing to extend the blessings You've given me. I want to please You and expand Your kingdom influence through the pathway You've placed me on. In Christ's name, amen.

Week 3

OWNERSHIP
versus
MANAGEMENT

Start

Welcome to group session 3 of Pathways.

Where was your first job? What did you do?

What's the difference between being an owner of a business versus being a manager? In what ways are the responsibilities different?

Before we begin, read aloud Esther 4:9-14 together as a group. The passage is summarized below.

When Esther received Mordecai's message about the danger to the Jewish people, she explained that she couldn't approach the king because Persian law meted out death to anyone who entered his presence uninvited. Mordecai answered by warning her that as a Jewess, her own life was in jeopardy and that God could save His people by another means if she failed. He believed her exaltation in the palace had a holy purpose. Esther's trust in God was the turning point in the story.

Watch

Complete this viewer guide as you watch video session 3.

God owns everything over which He rules, and He rules over everything.

Many people build the ladder of success and find it leaning against the wrong wall because it's not tied to something bigger than themselves.

God wants to put every Christian on display for the ownership of God and His kingdom.

When God gives you human success, human opportunity, it's for a kingdom purpose.

The closer you get to seeing, realizing, and prioritizing a kingdom connection to your human opportunities, the more God can reveal His pathway to your purpose, because His providence has put you there.

God is the owner of your life, your opportunities, your success, and your ultimate obligation is to Him.

The definition of a blessing in the Bible is to experience and extend the goodness of God to others.

If you can't answer the question how your calling is benefiting others beyond you, you haven't yet made a kingdom decision.

Video sessions available at lifeway.com/pathways or with a subscription to smallgroup.com

Discuss

Discuss the video with your group, using the following questions.

On the video Dr. Evans said, "God owns everything over which He rules, and He rules over everything." What changes about the way we go through life when we realize who's in charge of everything?

When you're climbing a ladder of success, how do you know whether that ladder is leaning against the right wall?

Esther 4:14 is easily the most famous verse in Esther and one of the most famous verses in all of the Bible. Have you ever heard this verse before? If so, in what context was it quoted?

What opportunities has God given you for a kingdom purpose? How are you making the most of these opportunities?

Dr. Evans said many Christians don't realize that God positions us where He desires for a much greater purpose. Why do you think so many Christians miss this truth?

How do you keep God's agenda central in your life so that you don't miss the connection between your opportunity and God's purpose for your life?

Dr Evans said the definition of a blessing in the Bible is "to experience and extend the goodness of God to others." Most of us understand blessing as experiencing the goodness of God. Why does true blessing call us to extend God's goodness?

Reread Esther 4:14. What would have happened if Esther had refused to use her influence as the queen?

What does it teach us about God that He's committed to His purposes with or without us? What does it teach us about God that He desires to use us in His purposes?

Read week 3 and complete the activities before the next group session.

Ownership versus Management

One reason we don't recognize God's goodness is that we confuse the means of His delivery with the source. Many times we think unless a blessing miraculously falls from heaven into our laps, it didn't come from God.

When you listen to music on a broadcast app on your smartphone, you can do so only because the smartphone is a method of delivery. There are no drums in the smartphone. No horns and no guitars reside in the equipment. The smartphone is only a conduit—a point of contact. Even when your smartphone stops working because your battery runs out, there's still music in the air. The smartphone simply receives a signal that comes from another source and delivers it to you. If you lose sight of that fact, you'll give the smartphone more credit than a smartphone ought to have. If you place too much weight on the medium, you'll forget the source. And if you forget the source, you'll feel no responsibility to Him when He asks you to sacrifice what you have for His greater good.

You'll be like the teenager who's reprimanded at home and grumbles to his parents, "I'm going to my room!" All the while the parent responds, "No, Son. You're going to *my* room. I just let you live there. And right at this moment, you're not going to my room. You're staying here until we've finished discussing this."

If you don't pay the bills, perform the upkeep, or purchase the items and furniture in the room, it's not your room. Similarly, the blessings and provision God has given you aren't yours. You're just a steward of all He has provided. As the owner of all, He reserves the right to ask you how to use His resources, even if that involves giving up something or someone in the process.

All of Esther's opportunities and gifts had been given to her "for such a time as this" (Esth. 4:14). God made her the queen so that when he desired to save His people, she would be in a position for Him to use her.

God is the owner; we're simply managers. Understanding ownership versus management will help you make decisions to serve God more readily.

This week's teaching draws out themes found in Esther 4:9-14.
Review this passage of Scripture before beginning your personal study.

◉ DAY 1 ◉

UNSHAKABLE KINGDOM

A number of years ago we decided to have our kitchen remodeled. The contractor came in and showed us some great plans. He showed us pictures of what the new cabinets would look like, samples of our options for wallpaper, and color cards with choices for paint. It was a glorious sight to see on paper what our new kitchen was going to look like. In fact, with so much excitement and anticipation about the new kitchen, we forgot about the process.

To get the kitchen remodeled, the old had to be torn out. The contractor had to tear up the floor, tear down the cabinets, move out the appliances, and sand down the walls. Things got so bad in our house that at one point we had to move in with our daughter to get away from the flying dust. We couldn't take it; we had to get out of there. But we wouldn't have been able to get a new kitchen if the old one hadn't been torn up first.

Many people want God to give them a new life, a new job, or a new situation, but they don't want Him to touch any of the existing details of their lives. If I had told my contractor that I didn't want him to touch anything, he would have told me that I didn't want to remodel. If I wanted new paint, a new floor, or new cabinets, none of that would have been possible if the old stuff hadn't been torn up first. We've got to trust God and give Him permission to tear things up in our lives so that He can make all things new.

List three of your common reactions or emotions during times when your life seems to be torn apart, dismantled, or disrupted. Why do you feel or react in these ways?

1.

2.

3.

Read Esther 4:9-14. What kind of disruption would Mordecai's revelation cause to Esther? What was he asking her to give up to help her people?

Read the following verse.

> *This expression, "Yet once more," denotes the removing of those things which can be shaken, as of created things, so that those things which cannot be shaken may remain.*
> HEBREWS 12:27

What makes God's kingdom fundamentally different from the kingdoms we build for ourselves? Why is pursuing God's eternal purpose always better than clinging to our own goals and benefits?

Sometimes God has to break us and remove from us that which we've come to rely on in order to rebuild us with spiritual strength, focus, and stamina. It never feels good when He's removing things we rely on for security, but if we'll trust the process, we'll see a greater good on the other side. Esther had attained a position of power and prestige. No doubt she had accumulated a plethora of material goods during her reign as queen. Yet in order to obey God's leading in her life, she faced losing them all if the king didn't extend his golden scepter.

Have you ever sacrificed or risked losing something to obey God? What was the result?

Read the following verse.

> *I urge you, brethren, by the mercies of God, to present your bodies a living and holy sacrifice, acceptable to God, which is your spiritual service of worship.*
> ROMANS 12:1

What are the attributes of living sacrifices, as compared to a dead sacrifices like the ones placed on the altar in Old Testament times? In what ways does God ask us to offer our bodies and lives as living sacrifices today?

God's specific purpose and calling require that we give ourselves to Him daily as a sacrifice. The word *therefore* at the beginning of Romans 12:1 signals that Paul was making an argument. He was saying, "In light of what God has done for you (see Rom. 1–11), offer your life as a sacrifice to God." Mordecai was telling Esther something very similar. He was asking Esther to take her blessings and sacrifice them for others.

Are you here for God? Are you willing to allow Him to use you to benefit others and build His kingdom? Or is this life only about you? If it's only about you, your goals are selfishness and self-preservation. You remove yourself from God's covenant covering of favor as you seek to grab as many treasures as you can stuff into your pockets. Your redemption is not just for you. God wants to use you for the benefit of others.

Read the following verses and identify attributes of a living sacrifice.

Psalm 51:16-17

Matthew 9:13

Ephesians 5:2

Philippians 2:5-7

Hebrews 13:15-16

Does sacrifice always involve giving up a tangible item or person? Why or why not?

How can offering ourselves as a sacrifice require us to change our attitude and demeanor toward others?

What are you willing (or unwilling) to give up or change to pursue God's kingdom purpose in your life?

We often limit our view of sacrificing for or obeying God to something we have to give up or stop doing. But Scripture tells us that showing love to others; sharing with others; praising and thanking God, even when we don't feel like it; and extending mercy, whether in word, thought, or action, are acceptable sacrifices. We can intentionally live with a spirit of sacrifice by modeling our choices after Christ's choices. The sacrifices and obedience we're called to may not always be as drastic or dramatic as Esther's risking her life by entering the king's throne room, but they're no less important. Be cautious not to devalue or belittle the obedience Christ has specifically called you to live out simply because it may not appear as grand as the sacrifices of someone you know or a character in Scripture. You're called to run your race and to walk faithfully on the pathway of your own God-ordained purpose.

PRAYER

Loving Lord, grow in me the ability to live as a sacrifice to You and for others. Help me show kindness, mercy, praise, generosity, and thanksgiving. Help me submit my thoughts, desires, and dreams to pursue Your heart and Your will for my life. In Christ's name, amen.

⊚ DAY 2 ⊚

YOUR USEFULNESS
IN THE KINGDOM

Sand on a beach is free. You can walk onto any beach and pick up a handful of sand at no cost. Pick up as much as you want, sit in it, and rub your hands through it. It's free. But if you want to put that same sand on a playground, it will cost you something. You'll have to go to the store and buy bags of it to cover the surface of the playground. Why? Because it's being used differently. It's no longer free.

If you want sandpaper to work on a project, that's going to cost you something as well. Yes, it's still sand—sand glued onto paper. But you'll have to go to a store and pay for a very small amount of this sand. Though it's essentially the same free sand, a higher value has been placed on it due to its intended use.

If you go to Silicon Valley, where people are busy making computer chips with sand, you'll find an even higher price associated with sand. That's the most expensive sand we could come across, not because it's different but because it's used differently.

One reason God often can't do much with His people is that He isn't free to use them. They're like free sand, with no purpose, intention, focus, or skill. They're just hanging out on the beach. God is looking for Silicon Valley saints—saints who've learned that their value is tied to their usefulness in His kingdom.

Describe a time when God directed you to do something specifically for Him that involved your intention, focus, or skill.

What did you learn by obeying God in that situation?

If a person walks around with one hundred dollars in his pocket but never uses it for what it was intended, it's just a piece of paper, meaningless until utilized for its purchasing power. God has assigned value to Christians. But until we live out our lives for their intended purposes, we walk around in a meaningless existence, valuable but not useful. A Christian life that isn't used for God's purposes is a life poorly spent.

Read Paul's direction.

> *Whether, then, you eat or drink or whatever*
> *you do, do all to the glory of God.*
> 1 CORINTHIANS 10:31

What does this verse reveal to you about the scope and breadth of your purpose in God?

Closely read Romans 12:2.

> *Do not be conformed to this world, but be transformed by the*
> *renewing of your mind, so that you may prove what the will*
> *of God is, that which is good and acceptable and perfect.*
> ROMANS 12:2

List the three characteristics of God's purpose for you.

1.

2.

3.

Recently, a single-service coffee maker in my kitchen stopped working. It would make all of the usual sounds when brewing a cup of coffee. It would light up as it should when brewing a cup of coffee. But no matter how long I stood there waiting for the cup of coffee to stream forth, nothing came out. You can imagine where this coffee maker wound up.

The coffee maker's usefulness determined where and how it was positioned. Likewise, your usefulness to the Lord and to His agenda determines the providential pathway He leads you on. Will you take the goodies and run? Or will you, like a wise manager, reinvest the assets of blessings He gives you to build greater opportunities for growth, influence, and impact?

> **Read Jesus' words in Luke 14:34. What happens to Christians when they lose their God-given purpose?**

> **Read Esther 4:8-11. What was at stake for Esther if she went before the king? Can you identify with her response? Why or why not?**

When Mordecai approached Esther and requested her to intervene on behalf of the Israelites, she balked. She paused. She stammered. There may have been many different reasons Esther didn't immediately respond. We may never know her exact reasons, but her response to Mordecai gives us a clue.

> **Mordecai ordered Esther to go before Ahasuerus (see v. 8). What motivated him to order her to go see the king? Do you think he may have anticipated her response?**

> **Read Esther 4:10-11. What are the main reasons Esther didn't want to approach the king on behalf of the Jews?**

How do we learn to push through fear and trust God's ultimate purpose? When have you been called to do this?

Initial reactions of fear can affect anyone. We're wired to protect ourselves. Many things in life may threaten or alarm us. However, discovering how to view the cause of our fears will give us the courage to push past our fears into faith. One time a dog was chasing my oldest granddaughter, who was about four or five years old. She was terrified. I don't think the dog was going to hurt her, but she didn't know that. She was crying and screaming as she ran to me as fast as her little legs would carry her. She was shouting my name: "Poppy! Poppy! Poppy!" That little girl was in a complete state of terror.

I ran to meet her and gathered her into my arms. She was huffing, heaving, and puffing, totally out of breath. The dog ran up to me, stopped short, and started barking. My granddaughter looked up at me and, noticing that the dog was no longer a threat, looked down at the dog and then up again at me. She looked back down at the dog and with renewed verve and vigor said, "Na-na-na-na-na!" Intimacy breeds confidence. When you're close to someone you love who has a lot more power than you do, you can piggyback on that power.

You can't overcome your fear through your own strength or courage, not at the level it takes to live in complete obedience to God. But as we'll see Esther eventually decide to do, when you seek to draw near to God in prayer, fasting, and intimacy, you'll discover a power greater than your fears.

PRAYER

Heavenly King, draw me close to You so that I'll have all I need to live in confident obedience to Your calling on my life. Show me the steps to take and empower me to take them. In Christ's name, amen.

⊙ DAY 3 ⊙

FOR SUCH A TIME AS THIS

A man used to lecture on child-rearing. A longtime professor, he had lectured through his single years and his parenting years, and his lectures had evolved over the years. When he was single, he began by calling his lectures "Ten Commandments for Parenting." After his first child he had to change the title to "Ten Hints for Parenting." After the second child it became "Ten Suggestions for Parenting." When he had his third child, he stopped lecturing altogether. Anyone who has raised children understands that you don't quite know all you thought you knew about parenting once you've had a kid or two. This is because children have been known to have minds of their own. Though the parent may be the authority, getting a child to do what you'd like them to do can prove difficult, especially after that child has grown into a young adult.

Mordecai wasn't Esther's father, but he had raised her. He knew her tendencies, personality, and preferences. He knew how she acted when she was happy and when she was sad. He knew whether she was naturally brave or naturally timid. And based on what he knew, he addressed her with regard to the Israelites' need for her intervention with a bit of stern parenting.

First, as we saw yesterday, Mordecai ordered Esther to go to the king (see 4:8). Esther hedged in her reply. She pointed Mordecai to the risk involved in complying with his order. When Esther continued to refuse to go to the king despite having been ordered by her elder family member, Mordecai brought up a very good point.

Read Esther 4:13-14. Summarize Mordecai's point in urging Esther to intervene.

How might this perspective change Esther's unwillingness to help the Israelites?

What does it teach us about God to recognize that His plan will succeed with or without our cooperation?

In Esther 4:13-14 Mordecai reminded Esther of her higher purpose in God's plan for the nation of Israel. He recognized that she mistakenly thought by not risking her life in approaching the king, she could save it. Yet her life had already been marked. She was a Jew. Thus, Mordecai attempted to shape her theology by informing her that if she didn't rise to this occasion and muster the courage to approach the king, God would raise up a solution through someone else.

No one, not even Esther, is indispensable in God's plan. If He can create the universe from nothing, He doesn't need any of us to accomplish His designed will. No matter how talented, rich, or powerful we are, God never limits the accomplishment of His plan to one person. He always has another option. He always has another person to accomplish His purpose.

Read Psalm 75:7 and Daniel 2:21. What do these principles suggest about your role in God's ordained plans and purposes?

How should these principles influence your decision making?

Although God may have preferred to use Esther in the king's palace and had positioned her to be used for His purpose through her role and status, He could also have easily found someone else. God is never boxed into a corner. He always keeps His options open in carrying out His promises.

One of the most dangerous things you can do as a kingdom disciple is to think too highly of yourself. Yes, God may have chosen to bless or position you for His use in His divine plan. The moment you demonstrate that He can't use you for His kingdom purposes, He can just as easily raise up someone else to replace you.

Disobedience to your kingdom calling puts you at risk of losing your kingdom calling. Wandering off the pathway of God's purpose puts you at risk of wandering in the wilderness of waste. God will never force you to fulfill your destiny. He will enable you to live out your purpose, but it's up to you, through your choices and character, to remain faithful to that purpose.

What are some factors that cause people to turn away from their calling?

Success is often the greatest deterrent to future success. Once someone tastes victory, whether it's in business, sports, or personal relationships, enlarged egos reduce drive and dependence on God. Pride swallows humility. Success can corrupt and can give birth to complacency.

Knowing these potential stumbling blocks, Mordecai had to make his point to Esther clear. In seeking to preserve the success she had attained up to that point, she was actually putting herself at the greatest risk of losing it. God had called Esther for this specific season and this specific need. If she chose to seek security over obedience, she could actually lose it all. Similarly, God has intentionally blessed and positioned you for His purpose.

When you choose to guard your blessings instead of extending them to others, you too become subject to Mordecai's rebuke. The greatest thing you could do to usher in a higher level of blessing in your life is to let go of the blessings you have now. Trust God with the outcome of His divinely ordained plan for your life as you recognize His true ownership and rulership over all.

PRAYER

God, I choose to surrender my life to You and to follow You in whatever ways You choose. Show me ways I've neglected my kingdom calling. Make me useful in Your kingdom. Show me how to help others through the blessings You've given to me. In Christ's name, amen.

⊙ DAY 4 ⊙

IF I PERISH

Many people quote Mordecai's rebuke to Esther as a life verse to represent prestige, power, and favor. Shirts, hats, mugs, and social-media posts proudly proclaim, "For such a time as this" (Esth. 4:14).Few people truly connect Mordecai's words with their context.

Have you ever quoted or shared the phrase "For such a time as this"? If so, in what context?

Esther was being scolded for her self-indulgent, self-preserving mindset. She was being reproved for living large and embracing royalty over service. Through those telling words, Mordecai was reminding Esther that she had been chosen to set her own interests aside, let go of her own ambitions, and boldly face an enemy. Esther was to risk her life and her legacy with no guarantee of a positive outcome. That's the "For such a time as this" Esther was challenged to accept. And that's the "For such a time as this" God also sets before you.

God has given you your job, position, resources, education, relationships, and many more blessings. He has granted opportunities for you to optimize for His kingdom purposes. He didn't place you where you are so that you could lounge around all day or post pictures of yourself on social media. He placed you where you are because you're in the midst of a battle, a war. You're in the midst of a seismic conflict involving good versus evil. To miss your kingdom assignment because you've become too caught up in your personal kingdom would be the greatest tragedy you could ever face.

Why is it so easy for us to miss God's sacrificial calling? How have you mistaken comfort for calling?

In what ways do we seek to remove risk and sacrifice from our contemporary view of following Christ? In what ways does our culture contribute to this tendency?

Mordecai's rebuke shook Esther, reminding her of the reality she lived in rather than the façade she had come to believe was real. Her response indicated that she understood what he was saying. Esther chose to take a risk in response to the need of her fellow Jews:

> *Esther told them to reply to Mordecai, "Go, assemble all the Jews who are found in Susa, and fast for me; do not eat or drink for three days, night or day. I and my maidens also will fast in the same way. And thus I will go in to the king, which is not according to the law; and if I perish, I perish."*
> ESTHER 4:15-16

Faith is risky business because you can't see it. The opposite of faith is sight. If you can see it, it's not faith. If you can know the outcome, it's not faith. If you can see the destination during every twist and turn on the pathway, it's not faith. Following a global-positioning system that outlines the entire path all the way to your destination isn't faith. Faith is acting on what you don't see. Faith is believing God's Word and taking one step even though that step is all you can see, simply because you believe God wants you to do it. Faith is taking a step without being assured of the destination.

Most of us don't mind taking a step when we can guarantee the outcome. But risky faith isn't based on a guarantee. Esther-faith isn't based on a guarantee. The greater the uncertainty, the greater the faith and dependence on God.

Read Esther 4:16. What was Esther's response to Mordecai?

Why do you think Esther asked everyone to fast for three days?

Based on this verse, how do we know Esther wasn't assured of a positive outcome?

Esther made the decision to risk her life for the good of others, specifically stating, "If I perish, I perish." She knew her husband's history. She knew he had a volatile spirit. She knew of Vashti's banishment. She knew the risk involved in approaching him uninvited. Yet Mordecai had reminded her that her obedience to God was necessary, not only for her own personal survival but also for that of her people.

Esther didn't know whether the king would hold out his scepter. But because she knew she'd been given a unique, royal opportunity for such a time as this to save her people from certain death, she chose to take that step of faith.

Throughout the Bible, people had to take risky steps of faith whenever God wanted to do something big through them. Their spiritual entrepreneurialism compelled them to take risks, acting on God's Word and His leading, in order to invest in a greater spiritual future. Esther was a strategic spiritual entrepreneur. She knew what she was up against. That's why she asked everyone to fast for three days and nights. If she was going to risk her well-being on their behalf, she needed them to invest in this battle as well. No war is ever won by one foot soldier. Esther was wise enough to realize this, and she sought spiritual support. She knew she needed to go before the heavenly King prior to approaching the earthly king.

Has there been a time in your life when you felt you needed to fast and pray about something? What did you do, and what were the results?

Have you ever fasted on behalf of someone else, or has someone fasted for you? What happened in that situation? Did the joint fasting have an impact on your relationship?

As we continue our study of the life of Esther, I want to encourage you to open your eyes and recognize God's purposes for you. God desires to use you. God wants to bless you. God chooses to empower you. But He also wants to see your faith in action. He wants to see you choose obedience over self-preservation.

With so much disintegration occurring in our homes, communities, and culture these days, we need to step out into the uncertainty of faith while following the certainty of the One who calls us. We need to restore hope and call people to transformed lives by modeling what it means to be a true kingdom disciple who actively engages in God's divine plan for the world.

When God reveals what He's asking you to do, be willing to do it. No matter the cost. No matter the potential for loss. No matter the risk. You've been called to the kingdom for a purpose much greater than your personal pleasure and gain. You've been called to the kingdom of God for such a time as this.

Whom do you know who's risking much for the sake of the kingdom? Stop and pray for him or her right now. Also pray that when called, you'll obey without hesitation.

PRAYER

Heavenly Father, I want to know Your will for my life, and I don't want my biases and desire for self-preservation to stand in the way of what You're asking me to do. I'm grateful for Your blessings and the open doors You've given to me. Help me use them to accomplish Your will and bring good to others in Your name. Show me areas of my life in which I'm holding on too tightly to what You've given to me. Show me how to maximize the resources You've provided—time, talents, and treasures— in such a way that You receive glory. In Christ's name, amen.

⊙ DAY 5 ⊙

THE RIGHT OF FIRST REFUSAL

Esther recognized that God had raised her to a position that would allow her to seek a remedy for her people. Mordecai's rebuke to her reminded her that God's will and God's ways were above her own. Therefore, she chose to step out in faith and approach the king. We saw in yesterday's lesson that before doing that, however, she asked the people to fast and pray with her for three days.

The combination of God's sovereign control—His ability to raise up whomever He wishes in order to fulfill His plan—and His allowance of our involvement within that control raises a great question on providence. Because God is sovereign and can do whatever He chooses to do, could we assume that what we do doesn't really matter? Such a worldview is called fatalism. Fatalism reflects a mindset that distances personal choice from consequences. But fatalism isn't biblical.

While Scripture emphatically teaches that God is sovereign, it also teaches that God uses people as part of the movements in history. God doesn't dismiss what we do; He uses it. Yes, God could have raised up someone else other than Esther to redeem His people. But Esther's choice to allow God to use her set in motion a legacy of good through her influence. Esther's influence thus stretched beyond this single incident.

Read the following verses.

> *God is not a man, that He should lie,*
> *Nor a son of man, that He should repent;*
> *Has He said, and will He not do it?*
> *Or has He spoken, and will He not make it good?*
> NUMBERS 23:19

> *I know that You can do all things,*
> *And that no purpose of Yours can be thwarted.*
> JOB 42:2

> *All the inhabitants of the earth are accounted as nothing,*
> *But He does according to His will in the host of heaven*
> *And among the inhabitants of earth;*
> *And no one can ward off His hand*
> *Or say to Him, "What have You done?"*
> DANIEL 4:35

What are three truths you learn from these passages?

1.

2.

3.

Even though God is sovereign, what are some ways He allows us to participate in His plans?

Our personal freedom of choice doesn't contradict or conflict with God's sovereignty. Although God could have used someone else if Esther had refused to help, His sovereignty provided the boundaries for her to move forward on her pathway to purpose. God's restrictions don't negate our freedoms; in fact, they enhance them.

For example, a tennis player isn't free to play tennis if there's no baseline. A baseball player isn't free to play baseball if there's no foul line. A football player isn't free to play football if there are no sidelines. Boundaries exist in athletic games to maximize the competition. The reason God allows boundaries is to create the opportunity for us to take full advantage of our freedom.

You can't be free without restrictions. A fish isn't free to roam the jungle. It wasn't made for that. A lion isn't free to live in the ocean because it wasn't made for that. Freedom is receiving the benefits you were created to receive. Freedom doesn't mean there are no boundaries. Freedom means that within God's ordained boundaries you can live out your purpose.

Esther chose to live out her purpose by remaining within the boundaries God had established.

List other boundaries that enable freedom to be experienced.

Why are boundaries so important? In what ways does God's sovereignty contribute to our ability to maximize our purpose in life?

A little boy was playing at a pond. His little toy boat was floating on the water and began to drift out where he couldn't reach it. Shortly a man came by and, seeing the boat out in the pond, picked up stones and threw them on the other side of the boat.

The boy didn't understand what the man was trying to do. The stones were causing quite a disturbance in the water and clearly weren't hitting the mark. Yet in time something interesting began to happen. As the man continued to throw stones into the pond, they created ripples of water that pushed the boat back toward where he and the boy were standing. Before long the boy had his boat once again.

God's sovereignty often doesn't make sense to us. His providential choices can seem as if they're missing the mark of what we'd like Him to do. Yet in His patience He continues. When we discover the power of obedience and faith in the face of what doesn't make sense, we'll reap the benefits of His providential movement in the circumstances and relationships in our lives. Like Esther, we can walk forward in the pathway to purpose predetermined by God's sovereign plans. But if we refuse to take that step, we can lose what had once been designated as ours. That's what happened to another member of royalty, King Saul.

Read 1 Samuel 15:1-11. How did Saul transgress the plans God had for Him? What was God's response to Saul's unwillingness to obey?

When Saul refused to obey, God chose another king in David (see 1 Sam. 16:12-23). What does this example teach us about God's commitment to accomplish His will despite our failure?

How can we develop an Esther-like attitude, which wants to obey God even when it's costly, instead of a Saul-like attitude, which seeks to save our own skin?

A common business term is called the right of first refusal. It gives a business owner the right to either accept or reject any new business proposals brought forward by the other entity named in the contract. This opportunity occurs before the other entity can take its business idea to a third party. Once the right of first refusal has been turned down, the other entity can approach another business with the new concept.

God felt sorrow over Saul's rejection of His calling. God assigns a calling to you. Yet like King Saul, you can disobey and refuse to carry it out according to God's commands and direction. In that sense you're turning it down, and God can assign it to someone else. But like Esther, you also have the right to live out your purpose in faith under God's overarching rule. The decision is up to you. God will never force you to follow the pathway He has created for you. But if you do, you'll discover that He has a plan that will bless not only you but many others through you as well.

PRAYER

Dear Lord, enable me to live like Esther with faith and wisdom to fulfill my purpose. Keep me from taking the path of King Saul, which merged personal gain and selfishness with Your purposes. Show me my pathway and light it with Your Word. In Christ's name, amen.

Week 4

FASTING and PRAYER

Start

Welcome to group session 4 of Pathways.

We're halfway through our study of Esther. What's one key takeaway you have thus far that you'd like to share?

What's your experience with fasting and prayer? Do you regularly practice these spiritual disciplines? Would you like to grow in these areas? If so, why?

Before we begin, read aloud Esther 4:15–5:14 together as a group. The passage is summarized below.

In response to the news from Mordecai, Esther requested a communal fast by all of the Jews as they petitioned God. She replied to Mordecai with courage and confidence in God's will: "If I perish, I perish" (4:16).

The prayers of God's people were answered when King Xerxes received Esther without incident. She invited the king and Haman to a banquet where she would make her request known. Once the guests had enjoyed their fill, Esther wisely paused and delayed her request for another day of feasting, no doubt at the Holy Spirit's leading. Haman left in a happy mood, but it was tempered by his fury for "Mordecai the Jew" (5:13).

Watch

Complete this viewer guide as you watch video session 4.

God has given us a point of contact with Him where earth can touch heaven and heaven can respond to earth. It's called prayer.

Throughout the Bible when there is a crisis, you will find men and women fasting along with their prayer.

Fasting is a deliberate abstinence from physical gratification of some kind for a period of time because of a greater spiritual need.

When you eat, you eat for the physical. When you fast, you're fasting for the spiritual.

God uses the Spirit to connect us with heaven, to bring the thinking of heaven down to the realities of history.

Don't miss out on the thinking of heaven because you're limited to the thought processes of earth.

While you may need a change in the physical, you need to make contact with the spiritual.

Sovereignty: God is in control.

Providence: God is manipulating the details to bring about His divinely ordained result.

Video sessions available at lifeway.com/pathways or with a subscription to smallgroup.com

Discuss

Discuss the video with your group, using the following questions.

What's your experience with prayer and fasting? Do you excel in practicing these disciplines, or would like to see growth? Explain.

At what points in your life have you been more drawn to fasting and prayer? What results did you see as you fasted and prayed?

Most people are more comfortable with prayer than with fasting. Why do you think that's true? Why don't we fast more?

Read Esther 5:7-8. The national fast caused Esther to be so sensitive to the Holy Spirit that she was able to adjust in the middle of her plans. Why would this ability be important to have in our lives?

Has the Holy Spirit ever led you to do something in a particular moment? What happened, and how did you see God work?

On the video Dr. Evans gave an example of the national news versus the local news. Fasting gives us the local news. Why is it so easy to become satisfied with the national news and never look for the local news?

What would it look like for us to fast together as a group? What's going on in our community that could benefit from a group fast?

If you fasted, what would you would abstain from? What would you hope to learn by abstaining from that item or practice in particular?

Read week 4 and complete the activities before the next group session.

Fasting and Prayer

If you've ever watched high jumpers in the Olympics, you probably realize there are two kinds. The regular high jumpers jump about seven feet by running and throwing their backs over the bar. But there's another kind of high jumper called a pole-vaulter, who jumps about eighteen feet. Pole-vaulters back up and look down the runway with the pole in their hands. They start running down the track, plant the pole in a hole in the ground, put all of their weight on that pole, and use the pole to lift them to a level they couldn't attain on their own.

Some of us have mountains—challenges we face that we see no way around, over, or under. These challenges have a crossbar we've tried to high-jump in the flesh. We've seen that mountain, backed up, and said, "Mountain, you aren't going to keep me down any longer." We grit our teeth with the power of positive thinking, New Year's resolutions, and vows not to repeat our mistakes. Then we take off and jump two feet when the bar is eighteen feet high.

Some of us have been jumping that same two feet for fifty years, and the bar is still up there. In fact, it keeps getting higher every year. Maybe what you need is a pole vault. You need something you can lean on as you approach your problem so that you can go higher than you could ever lift yourself. Maybe you need a pole that will help you jump over the mountain.

The pole vault for the bars in your life are fasting and prayer. Esther demonstrated this truth for us as few biblical figures have ever done. If you'll learn how to apply the principles she modeled, you can overcome anything and everything on the path to your destiny.

This week's teaching draws out themes found in Esther 4:15–5:14. Review this passage of Scripture before beginning your personal study.

⊙ DAY 1 ⊙

OUT OF LUCK

You may not notice how many times you hear the word *luck* in a day, but you probably hear it more than you may think. Our society seems to fixate on luck. People, even believers, regularly state, "You were lucky today!" Or if something goes wrong, they chalk it up to bad luck. Some people even hang a rabbit's foot on the rearview mirror of their car for good luck. Now that's always confused me. Obviously, if that rabbit lost its foot, it wasn't very lucky.

In contrast, the Book of Esther dismisses this concept of luck altogether, instead emphasizing the sovereign hand of God. Sure, sovereignty might look like luck, feel like luck, or even smell like luck. But it's not luck at all.

Sovereignty is the reality of God, who's always at work behind the scenes, ordering and aligning details and circumstances for His intended outcomes. God takes the good, the bad, and the ugly and makes them look as though they happened randomly. On the contrary, He either causes or allows events to happen that will ultimately usher in His will.

> **Read Proverbs 16:33. Do you ever find yourself chalking things up to luck or fate? What does this verse say about that idea?**

> **Read James 4:13-15. In what areas of your life do you need to intentionally include God and His perspective more in your planning and decisions? Why is it important to do so?**

Pathways

Review Esther 4:16. In what ways does Esther's call for national fasting and prayer reflect the principles found in James 4:13-15?

Providence places God behind the scenes of most things. He's like the ghostwriter of a book or the director of a movie. The results of His hands are seen far more than He is. While this fact is good in many ways, it can lead us to forget the level of His involvement in our lives. Then we make decisions based on our own understanding rather than relying on the One who knows best.

Esther knew who was in control. As we saw last week, she requested that her people fast with her for three days before she went to the king. On the third day of the fast, Esther put on her royal robe and entered the inner court of the king. This was the moment of decision. This was the time that would tell all. Would the king allow her to live, or was this the final curtain on her life?

Why do you think God usually works behind the scenes rather than being more direct and visible?

What are the dangers of forgetting that God is in control?

I imagine Esther's heart pounded within her as she quietly stepped into the inner court. Her knees may have felt weak beneath the weight of her worry. Where did she look? Did her eyes dart around in fear, or did she remain steady in confidence? What did her body language say before she ever opened her mouth?

Scripture doesn't give us the details about Esther's entrance, but Esther was human. Most of us would feel fear in a time like that. This reality makes Esther's action even more extraordinary. It also makes the king's response even more gracious.

Read Esther 5:2. What was the king's response to Esther's entrance?

Describe how Esther must have felt when the king touched the scepter.

Identify a time in your life when you faced a situation that could have gone really badly but didn't. How did you feel when you realized it was going to be OK?

The first part of Esther's challenge was done. She had stepped into the most dangerous situation of her life and had received a warm welcome. The king had graciously accepted her by extending the golden scepter. No doubt Esther felt relieved. But the plight of her people, including herself, still hung in the balance.

This had only been the first step. It wasn't the solution. A large portion of the pathway was still left to travel. Esther probably took a deep breath at this point, but then her mind probably raced forward to what she would say next. Every word matters when lives are on the line. That's why the three days of preparation by the people had been critical. By fasting and praying, the Jews had acknowledged God's ruling hand over all and had appealed to His great mercy. Now they were about to find out what He had in store for them next.

✳ PRAYER ✳

Lord, thank You that there's no such thing as luck, chance, or happenstance. Thank You that my life isn't a random occurrence without meaning or protection. Your guidance gives me the grace I need to pursue my purpose. Show me each step to take as I follow You. When I face fears or risks along the way, remind me to fast and pray. Remind me to ask others to join me in seeking You because we're united in Your body and intricately connected to one another. When we join together, give us wisdom and courage to face spiritual battles well. In Christ's name, amen.

⊙ DAY 2 ⊙

GROCERY SHOPPING ON AN EMPTY STOMACH

In yesterday's lesson we watched as Esther approached the king, no doubt full of fear. But placing her fear underneath God's rule and authority, she moved forward in faith. We also saw that the king responded to her in favor. What he said to Esther revealed a sentiment toward her of kindness and trust. He asked:

> *What is troubling you, Queen Esther? And what is your*
> *request? Even to half of the kingdom it shall be given to you.*
> ESTHER 5:3

Half of the kingdom? That's a lot of favor. Those thirty days without seeing each other obviously didn't reflect the state of the king's heart toward his queen.

I wonder what most of us would do if we were offered up to half of the kingdom by someone who had the power to give it. What would you do? Would you start making a list of all your favorite locations, activities, and merchandise throughout the kingdom? Would you lean back a little, put your hand on your hip, and say, "Well, OK, then. I'll take it"? Or would you, like Esther, let the greatest blessing of personal provision that's ever been offered to you slip away so that you could seek the welfare of someone else?

Have you ever been offered something that appeared to be great, but you turned it down for a spiritual reason? Describe what happened.

Did you have any regret for forgoing that blessing? Why or why not?

We get a peek into Esther's wisdom, restraint, and character in her response to the king's offer of up to half of the kingdom. Rather than go for broke, essentially taking the money and running, Esther considered the long-term play and exercised self-discipline. Rather than blurt out what was bothering her or even demand that her husband do something about the bully in the land, Esther chose wisely. She invited the king and that bully to dinner.

It's been said that the way to a man's heart is through his stomach. Esther seemed to know this maxim as well as anyone, so she decided to go straight for the heart of her king by going straight for his stomach.

Read Isaiah 55:8-9. How do God's ways differ from our ways? Why is it wise to trust in His ways over our own?

According to Psalm 27:11, how are we to know and understand God's ways in order to follow them? How often do you pray this prayer?

Identify a time when God's ways were clearly different from your own, yet you chose to follow Him. What was the result?

If you were having someone over to your house for dinner this afternoon, would you start preparing this morning? Sure, if it were a good friend or a family member. You might even skip the preparation and order pizza. But if it were a person of distinction from whom you needed a favor, you would probably start preparing at least the day before. Meals for distinguished guests require some forethought. Each dish has to be well planned out and prepared in advance.

Therefore, while the Jews and Esther had been fasting for three days, Esther simultaneously planned a feast. People say it's unwise to shop for groceries on an empty stomach because you buy too much food, but in the Esther's case it may have been very wise. No doubt the meal was carefully prepared and presented with the utmost attention to flavor and detail.

How did preparing the feast reflect Esther's faith that God would move the heart of the king?

Read James 2:18. How is faith displayed through action?

Esther needed divine insight for approaching a challenging situation. Her choice to fast and pray didn't mean she would lock herself in her closet and not come out. Rather, fasting and praying prepared the way for her to move forward in obedience.

The banquet was served on the very day Esther entered the king's inner court. The banquet Esther invited the king and Haman to attend had already been prepared by the time she invited them. The menu had already been chosen. Esther had done more than fast and pray. She had followed God's leading by taking action along the way. Her invitation to the king was couched in confident faith.

As you seek the Lord in fasting and prayer, be sure to couple those disciplines with actions that reflect His leading. Whatever you're facing right now, ask Him what He wants you to do as you continue to seek Him through prayer. Then, as you continue to pray, go ahead and implement what He directs you to do.

✳ PRAYER ✳

Father, increase my courage and faith so that I can move forward as You lead me. Help me overcome my fear of failing or of losing something I value as I obey you. Help me reflect my faith in my actions. In Christ's name, amen.

⊙ DAY 3 ⊙

HOW BADLY DO YOU WANT IT?

One reason we miss the so-called coincidences of God in our lives is that we don't have a raised antenna toward Him. We don't set aside the cravings of the flesh to seek answers in the spiritual realm. Then, when we fail to pick up spiritual signals and directions, we can't act on them. As a result, we operate according to our human viewpoint and our natural perspective.

Fasting and prayer lift our antenna into the spiritual realm so that we can pick up the picture from heaven we need to see in order to know what to do on earth.

Have you ever spent a significant amount of time in fasting and prayer? What were the results?

Why is fasting *not* an effort to manipulate God to give you the answer you want?

How can fasting change you or your perspective on what you're fasting for?

It's happened to me, and I'm sure it's happened to you. You're at work in a meeting, in a church service, or on the phone. All of a sudden your stomach growls, literally crying out for food. Not only do you hear it, but everyone around you also hears it. The message is clear: your body wants food, and it wants it now. Your body is trying to get your attention. The body's desire for food can be very strong.

Yet some things in life are more important than food. Some situations require a more-than-normal level of spiritual intervention. In these times it's not your hunger that cries out. It's your soul. God has given us resources for times of crisis like those Esther faced. God has given each of us the opportunity to fast and pray.

Fasting is deliberately refraining from physical gratification to achieve a greater spiritual goal. Throughout Scripture God's people fasted when they were in crises. When they desperately needed a breakthrough in their circumstances, their emotions, their relationships, their future, or their direction, they fasted. Fasting shows God that our need for Him is greater than our need for food.

Read Ezra 8:21-23. Why did Ezra ask his people to fast?

Read Luke 2:36-37. What's one reason to fast, according to these verses? Why should we consider fasting as a service to God?

Probably the greatest scriptural example of fasting occurs in Matthew 4, when Jesus went into the wilderness to be tested by the devil. After Jesus had prepared by fasting for forty days and nights, the devil came to Him and tempted Him to eat, but Jesus quoted Deuteronomy 8:3, declaring that man doesn't live "on bread alone, but on every word that proceeds out of the mouth of God" (Matt. 4:4).

Eating is one of the fundamental components of our humanity. We eat several times every day to satisfy our hunger and to obtain the nourishment and energy we need to survive. Yet occasionally, a situation arises that's more important than our next meal.

For example, when businesspeople are working on a major project, many professionals have a working lunch. They don't leave the office, because their work is more important than the meal. And if it's the last minute and they're rushing to meet a deadline, they skip lunch altogether because the task at hand is more important than food.

It's not just that way at the office. In many homes, caring for kids and running the household are nonstop jobs. Sometimes there's no time for the parent on duty to sit down and eat. For them, taking care of the kids' needs is more important than food, and the parent may not even realize they haven't eaten anything all day.

When we choose to fast, we deliberately show God that we're serious about getting His attention and that we're intently listening for His voice. We show Him that we're caught up in the priority of the spiritual realm. Fasting is intentionally choosing to place our hunger for God and our need for His intervention above any other need we have in the physical realm at that time.

Remember what Jesus said to the devil? We can't live just on food, because we need the Word of God even more. Fasting shows God and our stomachs that His Word is more important than food. When we fast, we give the Holy Spirit our full attention.

> **Read Zechariah 7:5-6. Record these verses in your own words. What happens when we fast but don't focus on God?**

> **How does this passage expand your thinking about what it means to fast and seek God?**

> **What can you do to put these principles into practice this week?**

Fasting sounds spiritual and holy, but it's hard for many believers to do. Whether it's fasting from food, an activity, social media, shopping, or talking too much or whether it's practicing the principles of mercy and compassion we just read about, fasting requires that you look beyond your own needs. Food is a great example of the way fasting takes your mind off yourself. If you're like me, you don't just enjoy food; you love it. When we eat, we're not thinking about God, our neighbor, or our loved ones. We're especially not thinking about anyone in need. We're thinking about how good our food tastes, whether we should have another serving, or whether we need to leave room for dessert. Zechariah 7:5-6 says when we eat, we do it for ourselves. When we fast, we do it for the Lord.

Fasting demonstrates our great need for God. It leads to a brokenness that shouts, "I can't do this!" A self-sufficient man or woman won't fast, but a desperate one will. The truth is, you can't live the Christian life in your own strength. You can't make things happen. You can't call on the flesh to defeat the flesh. By fasting, you demonstrate a true desire to grow closer to God and align yourself under His rule.

What challenges might you face if you fasted for an extended period of time?

Fasting makes your flesh weak because your body doesn't have the energy it regularly depends on. It's caught off guard; its defenses are down. But when you use the time you'd normally spend eating or doing another activity to read God's Word and pray, your spirit will grow stronger. When your flesh is weak and your spirit is strong, huge spiritual breakthroughs can occur in your life.

The question isn't whether fasting makes a difference. The question is, How badly do you want it? Maybe you're not desperate. Maybe you're not in a situation that has forced you to your knees in prayer. But if you are, I encourage you to fast, pray, and cry out to God to act on your behalf.

✷ PRAYER ✷

Loving God, give me the strength to fast, whether it's through giving up something in order to seek You or serve You or whether it's showing others a greater level of mercy and compassion. Give me the self-discipline I need to fast well. As I fast, Lord, reveal to me Your presence and enlighten me with Your guidance. In Christ's name, amen.

⊙ DAY 4 ⊙

STEPPING OUT IN FAITH

As we've seen this week, the first thing Esther did after she committed to move forward in a difficult situation was to admit that she needed God. She needed to talk to and hear from God because she didn't know how to overcome the obstacle ahead of her. From her example we've learned the important spiritual principle of fasting and prayer.

A second spiritual principle we glean from Esther's dinner invitation to the king is that she didn't rely on past victories or past strategies for present situations. Early in Esther's story we saw that she took very little into the king's presence on the night she was chosen to spend with him. She decided not to go all-out and create an atmosphere with trinkets and charms but rather to rely on the simplicity of her own sincere spirit to cultivate trust.

In contrast, when Esther invited the king to dinner, she prepared an elaborate banquet fit for a king—a king who knew well how to party and dine. His dinner-party standards were high, and Esther knew that.

Has there ever been a situation in your life when God has led you to change course? Did you make the change, or did you rely on the past approach?

Read Proverbs 3:5-6. What does it mean to "lean not on your own understanding" (v. 5, NKJV)?

One impediment that can keep you from witnessing a new experience of God's activity in your life is relying too heavily on His previous acts. Just because God does something one way the first time doesn't mean He will do it the same way the second time. In fact, He rarely repeats a method in the way He works. Yet far too many of us find comfort in seeking the repetition of past victories through past strategies rather than developing new areas of trust and faith in following the Lord.

Read 1 Samuel 30:8 and 1 Chronicles 14:14. What were God's answers to David in these verses?

What do these two situations demonstrate about the importance of seeking God for every decision?

Esther sought God because she needed His wisdom in that very moment for that particular circumstance. Then, when she heard from Him, she stepped out in faith. Literally. She walked into the king's inner court uninvited. Her step of faith brings us to an important point. Far too many Christians are waiting for God to do something, change someone, open a door, or defeat a challenge prior to doing anything themselves. Yet when God was getting ready to do something big for someone or for a group of people, He often asked them to do something first. After the exodus Moses held out the rod before the Red Sea opened (see Ex. 14:16,21). Later when the Jewish people were ready to cross the Jordan River into the promised land, the priests stepped into the water before it dried up (see Josh. 3:13). Essentially, God wouldn't move until His people moved in faith.

God wants to see that you believe Him, not just hear you say you believe Him. Faith is measured by footsteps. It's measured by your feet. Faith shows up in your walk, not just in your talk. It manifests itself through your life, not just through your lips. Faith makes itself known through your movements, not just your mouth. When there are no footsteps to back up your faith, it's not faith.

Read Hebrews 11:6. What's needed in order to please God? How would you define *faith*?

Has God ever asked you to take a step of faith? Describe what you did and what the result was.

Taking a step of faith always involves risk. If it didn't, it wouldn't be called faith. What would you think about a football player who bragged about his prowess during the week leading up to the game but chose not to actually play? What would you think if he conducted interviews or posted comments on social media about what he was going to do to the other team, but when the time came for the game, he chose to sit it out? You wouldn't think much of him, because he had made himself irrelevant. And you certainly wouldn't think twice about what he had said earlier in the week, because what truly matters is what's done on the field.

God isn't impressed by spiritual-sounding noise. He doesn't applaud the lofty words we say about believing Him, following Him in faith, and sacrificing for Him. The bottom line is that your faith is measured by the steps you take. The level of your faith is evident only by what you do, not by what you say.

Did it take greater faith for Esther to enter the king's inner court or to refrain from asking him for immediate action to help the Jews when he offered her half of the kingdom? Why did you answer this way?

Esther did more than offer the Jews mere sentiment about their predicament. She didn't offer them sympathetic words and a shrug of compassion. Nor did she passively place all the responsibility on God. Instead, Esther moved forward in faith. She saw a need, recognized that she could help meet that need, and took the risk necessary to become involved in the solution.

When God reveals a need to you, how will you discern what step of faith He may be asking you to take to bring about a solution?

✳ PRAYER ✳

Lord, I want to live with great faith. I realize this starts with a single step. Show me something to do that will demonstrate faith. Then meet me on the journey as You build this spiritual quality in me. In Christ's name, amen.

⊙ DAY 5 ⊙

GOD'S LEADING

Let's take a moment to review what we've covered so far in this Bible study. First, we've learned the lesson on sovereignty—that God is ultimately in charge of all that takes place. There's no such thing as luck, chance, or happenstance. We've also seen the power of courage in the face of fear. And we've observed that even during times of fasting and prayer, we need to move forward in faith. As God reveals what we're to do, we're to obediently take action.

Esther's dignified restraint when the king offered her up to half of his kingdom has taught us about the importance of self-discipline. We've also learned that God doesn't always guide us the same way in each situation, so to follow Him fully, we need to seek Him by asking for wisdom at all times. When we ask, He promises to give us wisdom (see Jas. 1:5).

Name some personal insights you've gained so far in this study.

In what specific ways do you plan to apply these insights or have you already begun to apply these insights in your life choices?

Read the following verses.

> *As they drank their wine at the banquet, the king said to Esther, "What is your petition, for it shall be granted to you. And what is your request? Even to half of the kingdom it shall be done." So Esther replied, "My petition and my request is: if I have found favor in the sight of the king, and if it pleases the king to grant my petition and do what I request, may the king and Haman come to the banquet which I will prepare for them, and tomorrow I will do as the king says."*
> ESTHER 5:6-8

How do we see God guiding Esther in these verses? How do we see Esther following His direction?

One way God guides us as we seek Him through fasting and prayer is by placing thoughts in our minds. Because God knows the end from the beginning, He can see a pathway when we can't. When Esther didn't know what to do, God gave her an idea. The second dinner would turn out to be more strategic than the first, but Esther wouldn't have known that when she entered the king's inner courts to invite him to the first banquet or while sitting with the king at that dinner. When the king asked her to state what she wanted—up to half of his kingdom—surely she must have been tempted to make known her appeal for her people. However, Esther refrained from revealing her true request because God guided her to invite the king and Haman to a second banquet (see v. 8).

Like Esther, we can see only the present and the past. We can't predict the future or people's responses to what we say or do. That's why it's absolutely critical to stay tethered to God, or abide in Christ (see John 15), in order to know the path to take.

Read Daniel 1:8-13. Describe what happened and the way God intervened to provide Daniel a way to overcome his circumstances.

God gave Daniel an approach that worked. After ten days the overseer saw that Daniel and his friends were more vibrant, strong, and healthy than the others, so the overseer allowed them to continue following their kingdom values. But God didn't give Daniel the idea until he had stepped out in faith and appealed to the overseer about his diet. Many of us are waiting for God to show up and do something in our lives, but God is waiting until we show up and step out in faith.

God doesn't always make sense, because we're finite and He's infinite. In Daniel 6 God didn't show up for Daniel until Daniel refused to pray to the king's statue—contrary to the king's command—and was cast into the lions' den. The Bible is replete with examples like this.

The reason many of us aren't seeing God maneuver and intersect the details of our lives in our favor is that we're not acting in response to God's leading. Instead of employing faith in action, based on what He has directed us to do, we're trying to manipulate the details of our lives ourselves. As a result, God's ideas aren't coming into our minds for dealing with the seemingly impossible situations we're facing.

In what ways does God call us to take risky moves in our culture?

How does God's guidance sometimes differ from our own cultural ideals of security and safety?

Describe a time when you wanted to move forward and act on something you were facing, but God encouraged you to show restraint. What was the result?

It's a good thing Esther had prepared the banquet, because the king didn't hesitate when he got her invitation.

Read Esther 5:5-6. What was the king's response to Esther at her first banquet?

Now review Esther 5:7-8. There's a pause between verses 7 and 8. Why is this significant? What might God have been doing during that pause?

Esther once again followed God's leading, continuing the strategy God had placed in her mind. There's a colon at the end of verse 7 in most English translations. In the original language of Esther, there's a distinct halt in the conversation. In other words, Esther started to make a request, then paused before continuing.

Rather than state her ultimate request, Esther asked the king and Haman to come to a second banquet to be held the next night. Keep in mind that Esther wasn't asking them to come back for leftovers. Elaborate preparation would normally be required for a banquet of this importance, yet Esther would have virtually no time to prepare. She put a plan in place to invite the king and Haman for dinner, not knowing what God was going to do between the first and second banquets.

Obedience doesn't require full knowledge of the way God is going to resolve a circumstance. Obedience means doing what God has asked you to do while leaving the unknown details in His hands.

In what area of your life could God be asking you to pause and consider Him? Are you listening?

✳ PRAYER ✳

Heavenly Father, thank You for Your wisdom. You say if I need wisdom, all I need to do is ask You for it. Lord, I'm asking now. Give me wisdom to know how to follow You more obediently and fully on the pathway You've set before me. Help me become a greater blessing to others in all I do and say. Show me the purposes for which You've placed me here. In Christ's name, amen.

Week 5

KEEP GOING

Start

Welcome to group session 5 of Pathways.

Do you find it easy to trust God?

In what circumstances are you more willing to trust God? In what circumstances would you be more reluctant to trust Him?

Before we begin, read aloud Esther 6 together as a group. The passage is summarized below.

The night after the banquet, the king was unable to sleep. The unstated reason for the king's insomnia was God's providence. To pass the sleepless night, servants brought the royal annals and read the entry that had been recorded when Mordecai saved the king's life (see 2:21-23). The king consulted Haman about the best way to honor Mordecai, but ironically, Haman's egotism unintentionally caused him to be the one to bring honor to his enemy. Once again we see God's providential hand at work behind the scenes.

Watch

Complete this viewer guide as you watch video session 5.

Your God and my God is the God of the unexpected.

God knows how to reach back and pull things forward when He's ready to use them because His pathways include yesterday, today, and tomorrow.

Keep your eye on God's timing. Keep going even though you don't know what's happening at the moment.

God is the God of details.

God in His providence is steering things—even small things—to accomplish a greater purpose.

Keep your eyes open because providence can sneak up on you.

The providence of God can use the dirt of hell to lift you to the pathway of heaven.

Discuss

Discuss the video with your group, using the following questions.

At the beginning of the video teaching, Dr. Evans cautioned against putting God in a box. How have you most often tried to box God in?

In Esther 6 God used something as seemingly insignificant as insomnia to change history. When have you seen God use something inconsequential to make a tangible difference in your life?

Until the king needed some midnight reading, Mordecai's help in saving the king's life went unnoticed, unpublicized, and unrecognized. What does this fact teach us about daily, ordinary faithfulness?

If God is the God of details, why do we have so many problems trusting Him with the details of our lives?

For what details do you need to trust God right now?

Earlier in this study we saw that our faith needs to be coupled with action. This week's study focuses on trusting God when we don't know what to do. How do these two ideas work together?

Dr. Evans mentioned that Christians should keep going in hard times because providence can sneak up on us. Why should the doctrine of God's providence fill Christians with hope and confidence?

What tempts you to doubt the confidence that God has given you in His Word?

It's important to be encouraged by the faith stories of others. Share a time when God has shown up exactly when you needed Him to.

Read week 5 and complete the activities before the next group session.

Keep Going

Florence Chadwick, a world-class swimmer, had already successfully swum the English Channel. Now she wanted to take on the twenty-six-mile course from Catalina Island, California, to the California mainland, which no woman had swum before.

Florence entered the Pacific Ocean with a number of boats surrounding her. Hour after hour she swam in thick fog. As darkness set in, she could barely see her hand in front of her face as she stroked. After swimming for almost 16 hours, she waved to the boats and said, "I can go no farther. I quit." They hoisted her out of the water and asked her, "Why can't you keep going?" She said, "Because I can't see. The fog is just too thick."

After getting on the boat, Florence discovered that she was only one-half mile from the coast of California. After all her hard work, she didn't quite make it, though she was ever so close.

Florence Chadwick decided to try again two months later. When she got into the water, the weather was bright and sunny, but after about 12 hours, fog set in once more, even worse than during her first attempt. Even though she couldn't see, this time she kept swimming. She not only swam from Catalina Island to the coast, but she also beat the world record by 2½ hours.

When Florence arrived at the California coastline, she was asked, "Last time you tried this, you quit. How did you make it this time?"

She said, "This time it was easy because I kept a mental picture of the California coastline in my mind. And as long as I didn't lose sight of where I was going, I could handle the trip getting there."

Traveling along the pathway God has for you often means traveling in the midst of dense fog. The end is rarely in sight. It's easy to want to give up when you don't know how much further you have to push through in order to reach where you hoped to go. But the lesson from Florence Chadwick and from Esther is to keep your eyes focused on God and His plan for you. Keep your heart tied to the truth that He has a plan for you, a good plan filled with a future and a hope (see Jer. 29:11). Trust His promises and His direction. Keep swimming. Just keep swimming. You're almost there.

This week's teaching draws out themes found in Esther 6.
Review this passage of Scripture before beginning your personal study.

⊙ DAY 1 ⊙

THAT NIGHT

Esther had just been given the second opportunity to ask for anything she wanted, up to half of the kingdom. The king waited on her next word, willing and able to grant what she asked. But Esther didn't ask for much. Yet again she asked the king and Haman to come to another banquet.

Timing is everything when it comes to arriving at your purpose. God is up to so much more than just what you can see in your immediate surroundings. When we began this study, I mentioned that God is the great puppet master. He's arranging, changing, maneuvering, and establishing connections so that when you arrive where you're supposed to be, your destination will be ready for you.

Esther 6 begins with these telling words:

> *During that night the king could not sleep.*
> ESTHER 6:1

The words *that night* are very important because this was the night between the two banquets. This was the night after Esther had previously turned down the king's offer to have up to half of his kingdom (see 5:3,6). This was the night when the fate of her people hung in the balance, and despite having two chances to request the king's intervention, she postponed asking.

Nevertheless, this night was necessary for events to unfold for her people's favor. Because this was the night when God moved the heart of the king as simply as "channels of water" (Prov. 21:1). This wasn't just any regular night. This was a very particular night when a very particular thing occurred: the king couldn't sleep.

Insomnia set in. The king tossed and turned, rolled over and complained. He sat up in bed. The king was meant to be awake because God had something He wanted him to know before the next banquet took place.

Read Proverbs 21:1. How should we feel to know that God is ultimately in charge of even the highest people in authority over our lives?

Describe what happened next in Esther 6:1-9. What did the king ask for when he was unable to sleep? What was Haman thinking when the king asked him how he should honor someone?

God's providence is tied to time. The Book of Esther covers years, even decades. Providence weaves through time and circumstances like a spider carefully crafting its web. Each movement may not appear to lead to anything significant until the entire web has been completed, but every movement and motion matters. This is why you must trust God's heart even when you don't see His hand.

Mordecai had saved the king but had never been recognized. Have you ever been denied the recognition you felt you deserved for helping someone? How did you respond?

Why should we trust that God is always working even when it seems as though He is absent?

God sits outside time, while we live within it. Describe the tension these realities sometimes create for our faith.

During his sleepless night the king requested the reading of the chronicles. This book was a record of significant events during the king's reign. In them he learned of Mordecai's heroic act in saving his life. What came next, though, is a sequence of events we might find in a Hollywood movie. Consider the irony. The king asked Haman how to honor the very man Haman wanted dead without revealing to Haman that he was referring to Haman's enemy, Mordecai. This is the stuff of great cinematic plotlines.

There Haman stood, his head enlarged with pride, his chest puffed out, and his shoulders squared, casually listing a number of things he wanted the king to do for someone he would want to show honor. Of course, Haman thought that someone was himself. But his assumption couldn't have been further from the truth.

Not only did Haman guess wrong about whom the king intended to honor, but he also guessed wrong about his own role. Rather than being the one led through the streets in great esteem, Haman now had to lead Mordecai through the streets publicly calling people to honor him. This twist of fate came at the hands of God Himself. Through Esther's obedience in inviting the king and Haman back for a second banquet, God utilized the time between the meals to orchestrate an unexpected turn of events.

Never in Esther's wildest imagination could she have come up with the idea of Haman's parading her uncle around to bestow honor on him. That's about as absurd as a military general who orders the people of Israel to walk around a city's walls for seven days in order to defeat the military camped in it (see Josh. 6). But that's how God works. He works above and beyond our wildest imaginations. That fact is why your progress on your pathway to purpose is largely tied to your obedience to Him on a daily basis.

If Esther had felt afraid and decided to manufacture her own solution by accepting the king's second offer of anything up to half of the kingdom, there would never have been a "that night" (Esth. 6:1). Far too many times believers rush ahead of God because we can't see what He has in store. And we can't see what He has in store because it's often beyond our wildest imaginations.

Why is it critical to wait on God's timing of events when pursuing His purposes for you?

Have you seen God come through for you in a way that was unpredictable or beyond your wildest imagination? What happened? If not, ask God to work in your circumstances to create such an opportunity.

Haman's plan to publicly display brutality against Mordecai turned around to become an even more public display of favor. This reversal highlights one area of God's sovereignty and providence we often overlook. God is a God of intersections. He connects events that don't look connectable. He dislodges and alters situations that appear set in stone. He maneuvers through the maze of what appears to be unrelated occurrences. Because we can see only what's immediately before our eyes, we rarely get a glimpse of how He works. But in stories like Esther's, even though His name doesn't appear in the book, God offers a full view of who He is and the way He orchestrates His will.

God always has a plan in play, even though He often speaks to us in ways we don't recognize. That's why when we fail to set spiritual priorities in our lives, we'll often fail to pick up on the signals that are all around us. When the receiver is off the hook, we can't answer the call. We can't connect the dots. We can't see the forest through the trees. Failing to detect signs of God's work can prevent us from traveling the full pathway to our purpose.

✳ PRAYER ✳

Jesus, I want to see Your hand mightily work in my life. Help me abide and grow in my intimacy with You so that I can discern and respond to Your activity in my circumstances, opening the door for You to work wonders in the challenges I face. In Your name, amen.

⊙ DAY 2 ⊙

CHASING DONKEYS

Providence means God intentionally stops, starts, delays, quickens, directs, moves, changes, allows, blocks, and transforms as part of His sovereign plan. And He does so on purpose to intersect people, thoughts, and processes with His intended aim. We see this pattern throughout the stories of Scripture. Let's take a look at an example that occurred in the life of another royal, Saul, before he became king.

Read 1 Samuel 9:1-6. Describe the situation Saul found himself in.

What are some common emotions Saul must have felt while he was searching for the lost donkeys?

Have you ever been in a situation in which you felt lost, hopeless, or lacking in direction? Is it possible that God could have a purpose in what looks like aimlessness? Why or why not?

Read 1 Samuel 9:15-20. What had God told the prophet Samuel about Saul prior to his coming to meet him?

While Saul had been wandering around looking for his lost donkeys, God had instructed the prophet Samuel that He would send him the future king of Israel the very next day. If Saul hadn't lost his donkeys in the first place, his pathway wouldn't have approached the proximity of the prophet. God turned what appeared to be an unfortunate event into a divinely designed promotion.

Often we may feel we're aimlessly wandering around, unable to connect the dots of where God has allowed us to go and what He has allowed us to do. But when we stay committed to Him and His Word, He can bring about order from what looked like confusion. Yet unfortunately, in our frustrations we sometimes want to give up. First Samuel 9:7 tells us Saul's initial response when his servant urged him to go see the prophet Samuel:

> *Behold, if we go, what shall we bring the man?*
> *For the bread is gone from our sack and there is no*
> *present to bring to the man of God. What do we have?*
> 1 SAMUEL 9:7

Because Saul couldn't make sense of the situation, he wanted to turn around and do what was most logical to him: return home to his father. But because he listened to wise counsel and sought the advice of the prophet, God intersected the situation with His plan to promote Saul to king.

Read 1 Samuel 10:1,24. Summarize what happened to Saul.

We often see the way God was working in our lives only in hindsight. Why is this pattern actually good for us?

At just the right time, God intersects people and events with His intended aim. Believing this truth will free you to live in a depth of faith that allows for what you can't explain. This faith will enable you to move forward even when you feel you're being overlooked. In the moment, Saul didn't have the ability to realize what was happening. When Mordecai sought to protect the king, he didn't know how God would use that deed. This kind of faith recognizes that God works behind the scenes to arrange events until the proper season brings them to fruition.

Read Galatians 6:9 and Colossians 3:23-24. What encouragement do these verses provide when we labor for the Lord but don't immediately see results?

Nothing ever goes to waste in God's economy. No kind deed you perform. No act of devotion or sacrifice for Him. God keeps a record of all you do and rewards your faith and your actions. That reward may not take place in the time frame you expect it to, and some rewards won't come until heaven, but God is both just and faithful. He sees you, just as He saw young Saul and just as he saw Mordecai.

Don't allow yourself to get frustrated and upset when it looks as if other people are blocking your progress in life or creating problems for you to deal with. Why? When you align yourself under God's rule, He can change things in a moment. He can turn circumstances around. He turned Mordecai's situation around in less than twenty-four hours. The man was supposed to die the very same day he wound up riding on the king's horse through town.

When God is ready to move, He doesn't need a lot of time. He can move suddenly. Furthermore, He doesn't need anyone's help. In His providence God can take forces in your life that were meant to harm you or keep you from moving forward and can use them to usher you into your destiny. God is always at work when circumstances appear out of control. Always.

Is yielding to God's providence an excuse to do nothing? Why or why not?

According to Proverbs 16:7, what's required for difficult people to be at peace with you?

God is the God of reversals. He can make your enemies your footstool and can cause them to be at peace with you. But these results are conditioned on your alignment underneath His rule and authority in your life. His Word must govern your thoughts and actions. When that happens, buckle up because you're about to witness the extraordinary hand of God move in your life., just as it did with Mordecai. The same man who had set out to hang him on gallows was now leading him around town on the king's horse. God is the God of reversals.

Read Romans 8:28. What does this Scripture teach about God's providence?

What assurance can a Christian have in knowing that all things work together for their good?

The same God who sovereignly intervened to flip that script is the same God who knows how to address whatever or whomever you're facing. He can alter your situation and reverse it for your good and His glory. If you'll let go of the pain that comes from confusion, release the distrust that rises from the dust of disappointments, and replace both with trust in the providential heart of God, you'll see Him reverse circumstances in your life you thought could never change. He can turn things around, even overnight.

Are you facing a situation you need God to turn around? Pause and take time to pray and ask God to intervene. Also ask Him to give you wisdom and patience not to try to intervene yourself.

✳ PRAYER ✳

Dear Lord, I want to witness Your hand moving in my life.
I need You to turn around particular circumstances and
obstacles, so I call on You to do so, asking You to guide me
along the path You have for me. In Christ's name, amen.

⊙ DAY 3 ⊙

NO MORE WORRY

The average person is born with more than one hundred thousand hair follicles on his or her head. Sure, a large number of those hair follicles no longer produce hair by middle age, but we all get a fair start. Multiply that average number of hair follicles by seven billion people on the planet, and you're now in the octillion range of mathematical computation. When most of us think of octillion, we think of that slimy creature living in the sea, not a number far beyond our natural ability to compute. Yet God says not one solitary hair falls from your head with which He isn't fully acquainted (see Matt. 10:30; Luke 12:7).

This God is so much bigger than we often give Him credit for. He's so much more able than we often realize. He's so much more sovereign in the daily workings of our lives than we often dare to fathom. He's so brilliant that He can make sense of details and events that appear to be totally unrelated, disconnected, and random. He can put a billion-piece puzzle together in less time than it takes us to blink.

It's this greatness of God we need most when life has become a mess. It's this strategic sovereignty we must rely on when life no longer makes sense. It's this control by our Creator we must trust when circumstances appear chaotic. As children of the King, we're called to believe in this doctrine of sovereignty because that's how we live by faith. In times when things aren't going our way, we believe in this God who strings together the incomprehensible in order to make sense of the senseless.

Yet even so, it's easy to feel in uncertain times that if we don't take care of our problem, it won't be taken care of.

Why do we at times doubt that God can't take care of our daily needs?

In what ways do your thoughts or actions indicate that you might not truly believe God can or will take care of every issue you face?

Read Jesus' words.

Who of you by being worried can add a single hour to his life?
MATTHEW 6:27

How did Jesus approach the subject of worry in this verse?

To worry is to question God's integrity. In Matthew 6:31-32 Jesus said the Gentiles—pagan people who didn't know God—were concerned with what to eat, drink, and wear. God's people, who know Him and have a relationship with Him, shouldn't live or think the same way as those who don't. God is insulted by our worry.

If we, who know God, are constantly worried, what does our worry communicate to unbelievers about our confidence in God?

Kingdom life requires faith. Faith is trusting that what God says is true, even when we can't understand it or see its connection to our circumstance. Faith is taking steps that demonstrate what He has said is true. It's acting as though something is so even when it's not so in order that it might be so, simply because God said so. Faith requires risk beyond reason because we trust that God knows what He's doing.

How does trusting God reduce worry?

Read Psalm 56:3. What's the antidote for fear?

Esther is often applauded for her bravery and courage. She's frequently remembered as a woman who was strong enough to risk her life by approaching the king. But Esther was no stoic warrior. She had fears to overcome. She had worry to face. As we'll see, Esther 8:3 reveals that when she asked for the king's intervention on behalf of her people, she literally wept at his feet. That's a position of submission and humility. Esther's tears reflected the essence of her humanity. Yet regardless of all she must have felt inside, she acted in complete faith.

Perhaps even more admirable than entering the king's inner court uninvited was Esther's willingness to follow God's leading. Her faith gave her wisdom, discretion, and restraint. God was busy setting up all of the pieces of the grand drama and putting everything in place, but He still needed Esther to walk by faith. He needed someone who was willing to trust Him with a pause. He had to have someone who was willing not to rush ahead and try to solve the problem herself. He had to have someone who, when asked what she wanted up to half of an entire kingdom, could stick to the plan and simply say, "I want you to come to dinner" and then, when asked the same question again, could reply, "I want you to come back for dinner once again." God needed someone who was willing to submit her personal strategy to His Spirit's reign.

What worry, obstacle, or delay in your life do you need to turn over to God?

✴ PRAYER ✴

Heavenly Father, help me trust that You're in control of all of life. Have patience with me and lead me to see Your care for me daily. Show me how to stop worrying and follow Your Spirit's leading in every step I take. In Christ's name, amen.

⊙ DAY 4 ⊙

YOUR PERSONAL GPS

The Holy Spirit is your very own global-positioning system. His role involves guiding you to where you need to go and leading you to speak when you should speak up or to be silent when you should remain silent. He opens doors and shows you that they're open. Or He closes doors and seeks to prevent you from pushing on through. The Holy Spirit has been given to you in such a personal way that you have a direct link to the mind of Christ Himself.

> **Read the following verses and identify the roles of the Holy Spirit.**
>
> **John 14:26**
>
> **John 16:13-15**
>
> **Acts 11:22**
>
> **Acts 16:6-7**

As followers of Jesus Christ, we have no excuse for not knowing which way to go and what pathway to take. Christ's death, burial, and resurrection provided us with all we need for the ongoing presence of the Holy Spirit to guide us each step of the pathway to God's purpose. The Holy Spirit is the antenna that allows us to receive the signal God sends. He's the conduit that applies God's truth to our lives.

The Holy Spirit directs not only what we do but also when we do it (see Acts 11:22; 16:6-7). At times God won't give us the freedom to move forward on something, nudges us to move forward more quickly than we thought, holds us back from saying what we feel, or leads us to say something we never thought we would. The Spirit connects us to Jesus and gives the freedom or the restriction we need to remain on the path of God's will. Yet if we don't have a spiritual antenna connected to God's presence, we won't pick up on His leading. We won't know which step to take and when to take it.

Read the following verses.

*A natural man does not accept the things of the Spirit of God, for they
are foolishness to him; and he cannot understand them, because they
are spiritually appraised. But he who is spiritual appraises all things,
yet he himself is appraised by no one. For "who has known the mind of
the LORD, that he will instruct Him?" But we have the mind of Christ.*
1 CORINTHIANS 2:14-16

**According to these verses, who has the mind of Christ? What does
the mind of Christ enable a person to do?**

If you choose to live with a worldview rooted in secular thinking, you'll interfere
with God's program for your life because you'll move when He doesn't want you
to move, and you won't move when He wants you to move. You'll speak when He
doesn't want you to speak, or you won't speak when He wants you to speak. If
your receiver is turned off, you can't discern how to pick up heaven's signal. Then
you won't know which step to take in the right direction. It would be like trying
to hike up a mountain at night without a light—dangerous, disastrous, and deadly.
The Holy Spirit's work in your life illuminates God's guidance as you travel this
journey called life.

One of the main reasons you and I need the Holy Spirit's illumination is that God
often acts counterintuitively to the way we think and plan. Many times God uses
negatives to accomplish positives. He uses what appears to be something bad to
bring about something good. He even uses the devil to achieve His righteous goals.
And if He's willing to use the devil to bring about His intended outcomes, He's
willing to use devilish people as well.

Read Matthew 4:1. Why did the Holy Spirit lead Jesus into the wilderness?

Why would the Holy Spirit lead us into circumstances that don't seem beneficial or safe from our perspective?

What do you think God's purpose is in allowing us to face challenges, temptations, or difficulties in life?

Spiritual development often comes through the challenges we face. Just as athletes can't improve in their sports without the pain of working out and practicing, we can't develop the spiritual muscles of faith, trust, belief, and resilience without testing. At times that means the job of the Holy Spirit includes leading us into situations designed to strengthen our character. When we work with God in these circumstances instead of against Him, we can overcome them at the speed with which Christ overcame the devil in the desert.

Read Matthew 4:1-10. Briefly summarize Jesus' responses to all three of the devil's temptations.

1.

2.

3.

Now read Matthew 4:11. What did the devil do when Jesus responded as He did?

Jesus responded to each challenge and temptation by relying on the power and truth of God's Word. He didn't break into a long speech, take a workshop, make a list, or draft a New Year's resolution. His response quickly and concisely demonstrated the power of God in that situation. All the devil could do was leave.

After Satan left, angels came and ministered to Jesus in order for Him to regain His strength. Following God isn't a lifelong party. Sometimes you feel drained and need to be ministered to. Sometimes challenges seek to defeat you or take you off course.

As we saw earlier, Esther laid it all on the line. But in these times of trial, God ushers in His greatest interventions. He sent angels to minister to Jesus. And He gave Esther the answer for which she had pleaded. If you'll remain faithful as the Holy Spirit leads you, whether through good times or hard times, you'll discover that God is there to meet you, strengthen you, and encourage you just when you need Him most. Trust the process. He knows exactly how to take you to the greatest possible fulfillment of your purpose if you'll stay on the path He has sovereignly ordained.

Trusting in sovereignty doesn't mean we don't risk. Often it means the opposite. What risk might God be asking you to take for the sake of His kingdom?

How do we stay in sync with the Holy Spirit so that we can respond to His leading, even when it's hard or risky.?

✳ PRAYER ✳

Father, thank You for the gift of the Holy Spirit, whom You've given to me as a guide, helper, minister, and encourager. I often neglect to acknowledge the Spirit's presence in my daily life and choices, to my detriment. I ask that You'll remind me to stay connected to and filled with the Spirit so that the full manifestation of His leading and care will be evident in my life and in the lives of people around me. In Christ's name, amen.

⊙ DAY 5 ⊙

SUDDENLY

I love the lessons we've learned from the life of Esther, Mordecai, Haman, and the king. These stories provide a unique vantage point for seeing ways God guides us and arranges events behind the scenes. At the beginning of this week's lesson, we saw that the king couldn't sleep on the very night Esther and Mordecai needed him not to sleep. God kept the king awake long enough to get more information on Mordecai—information that would drastically change his view of him and the Jewish people.

Next we chased some donkeys with a guy named Saul, who, as a result of this chase, would be named the king of the Israelites. Through Saul's story we discovered how God works in the meanderings of life, connecting them with other people, places, times, and events in order to bring about His intended plan.

After that we considered the amazing truth that God has given us His Holy Spirit to guide us along the pathway to the destiny He has appointed for us. The Spirit's role is tell us which steps to take, which ones to avoid, and how to move forward on the path. We also saw that the Spirit sometimes allows us to face challenging situations because in them we get to witness God's deliverance and power and have an opportunity to experience spiritual growth.

Today we're going to look at one of my favorite words in the Bible: *suddenly*.

Read 2 Chronicles 29:36. Summarize this verse in your own words.

Read Acts 16:25-26. What situation were Paul and Silas in? How did God address it?

One reason the Book of Esther was recorded was to demonstrate God's unique way of orchestrating events and circumstances. He normally doesn't work things out straightforwardly. Rather, He weaves as we wait. He positions as we pause. He maneuvers as we move. Then when the time comes, as it did for Esther, He sets the stage. Suddenly. In less than twenty-four hours God flipped the script, and the curtain rose on a brand-new scene.

Throughout Scripture God suddenly moved to arrange, rearrange, position, and promote His plan. Waiting on God means we're waiting for Him to put details together in the perfect timing for His purpose to come about. God is a God of *suddenly*.

Has God ever acted suddenly in your life or in someone's life you know? Describe what happened and what was learned through it.

Is there any area of your life in which you want God to act suddenly on your behalf? Take a moment to pray and ask for His intervention. Also ask the Holy Spirit for wisdom for what you should do, say, not do, and not say in the situation. Record your thoughts.

Read God's words in Isaiah.

> *I declared the former things long ago*
> *And they went forth from My mouth, and I proclaimed them.*
> *Suddenly I acted, and they came to pass.*
> ISAIAH 48:3

Does God require a particular length of time to bring to pass what He intends? Why do we try to place time constraints on God?

Pathways

I wish I could tell you how much longer you'll have to wait for change to come to your situation. I wish I could tell you how much longer you'll be disrespected or overlooked in your job. I wish I could tell you how much longer you'll be treated unjustly. I wish I knew how long the waiting game would be in God's plan. But I don't. There are too many pieces of the puzzle. There are too many people on the pathway. There are too many processes in the plan.

I can tell you that when God shows up, He will often come suddenly and in an unexpected way. He often lets things get worse before they get better. Sometimes He allows you to go all the way to the end—to hit rock bottom—so that you'll discover that He's the Rock at the bottom. In doing so, He builds your faith muscles and strengthens your spirit. He also gets the glory and the praise because only He can produce a miracle from a mess.

According to Matthew 15:28, how long did it take for the woman's daughter to be healed?

What did Jesus identify as the root of that healing?

Describe the link between faith and God's sudden movement in our lives. How is faith demonstrated?

When the kids were much younger and I was in seminary, my wife stayed home to take care of the two children we had at that time. I worked while going to school full-time, but the income wasn't enough to adequately provide for our family. One morning before heading off to school, I sat down with my wife for our morning devotion together. She broke into tears as she shared that she couldn't go on with the bleak amount of money we had.

I felt like a failure at that time and committed to do all I could to take care of my family, even if that meant quitting seminary and working full-time. But before I quit, I asked her to give me twenty-four hours in which we would both seek God for His wisdom and leading. I asked her, "How much money would you need in the next twenty-four hours for you to believe God is leading me to stay in school?"

"Five hundred dollars" was her reply. In the 1970s five hundred dollars was a lot of money. But when I arrived on campus just a few hours later, I opened my mailbox to discover an envelope containing five one-hundred-dollar bills. I hadn't told anyone about our request to the Lord that morning. Only God knew. But that's all who has to know. Because God can change things suddenly.

God often allows us to get backed into a corner, where we no longer know what's going on or how to solve our challenges. He does so in order for us to discover that He alone is God. But if your spiritual antenna isn't up—if you're thinking worldly thoughts, living worldly values, and making decisions based on your own insight— you won't be able to pick up the signals of His Spirit. You'll miss the leading that's necessary to take you along the pathway of providence.

✳ PRAYER ✳

Lord, I want to see You move suddenly in the challenges I'm facing. I commit my heart and mind to You and seek Your will and provision, knowing as I trust in You, I can also rest in the confidence of that trust. You can move quickly. You can bring about change. I believe that, and I ask for that. In Christ's name, amen.

Week 6

DIVINE REVERSALS

Start

Welcome to group session 6 of Pathways.

If you're a sports fan, when have you seen a big reversal in a game?
How exciting was that to watch?

Have you ever watched God do something surprising and unexpected? When?

Before we begin, read aloud Esther 7; 8; 9:20-27 together as a group.
The passage is summarized below.

Not only did Mordecai get the best of Haman, but Esther also outsmarted him.
On the following day Esther assembled her guests for the second banquet, during
which she revealed her request.

Haman begged for the queen's mercy, thus breaking protocol with the king's harem.
He magnified his folly by stumbling to her couch, creating the appearance of impro-
priety and thereby sealing his doom with the irate king.

Esther successfully pleaded for the king's assistance to avert disaster for her people.
The royal decree Mordecai wrote answered Haman's evil decree by giving the
Jews the right to defend themselves. The thirteenth of Adar, the day that had been
planned for the Jews' destruction, was exchanged for the two-day celebration of
Purim because of the Jews' conquest.

Mordecai took Haman's place as second to the king. The author repeated the subse-
quent victory of the Jews because it established the Feast of Purim on the traditional
calendar. The feast was named Purim because of the pur ("lot") cast by Haman
earlier in the story.

Watch

Complete this viewer guide as you watch video session 6.

God turns things around and flips them from where they were to where they ought to be to fulfill His purpose for us and to bring greater glory to Himself.

A social reversal

A political reversal

A legal reversal

When God moves, He can use individuals to affect whole societies and to transform whole nations.

God raises up people at strategic times to effect His purposes, to accomplish His program, and to guide us to our purpose.

An emotional reversal

Our emotions are affected by the information we're fed.

Look for where God is moving, even when you don't see God directly.

A spiritual reversal

It's never just about you. God wants to introduce other people to Himself through you.

God is after great reversals because He's after spiritual transformation.

The greatest reversal of all is Easter Sunday morning.

Video sessions available at lifeway.com/pathways or with a subscription to smallgroup.com

Discuss

Discuss the video with your group, using the following questions.

This session focuses on the idea that our God is a God of reversals. What reversals have you observed during the time you've followed the Lord?

Dr. Evans taught that God can use individuals to bring about change for a whole society. What's once tangible way God is using you to change the world around you?

If God can bring change through individuals, how much more can He do through the collective work of the church?

Read Esther 8:16-17. God gave the Jews an emotional reversal. Why are we sometimes unwilling to trust God with our feelings? Why should this reversal give us confidence that God cares about our emotions?

Dr. Evans discussed the value of looking to find where God is moving, even when we don't see Him directly. How do we increase our sensitivity to God and His activity?

Where do you see God moving and bringing about a reversal right now?

Reread Esther 8:17. God's work in your life isn't just about you. How can you use what God is doing or has done in your life to help other people see the glory of His name?

Why is Easter Sunday the ultimate reversal? What does Easter Sunday teach us about the nature and providence of our God?

What's one big takeaway for you from the Book of Esther as we come to the last week of study?

Read week 6 and complete the activities before the next group session.

Divine Reversals

Out with the old and in with the new. It's a cliché most of us are familiar with. This phrase is meant to communicate the importance of moving forward with the times and leaving behind what has become outdated. I have a flip phone. In this age of tablets and smartphones, I know my ancient instrument of technology must seem useless. All of my staff tries to communicate with me through text messages and emails. Honestly, I'd rather just stick to paper memos and handwritten notes.

The reason I haven't embraced the newer technology is that I'm simply too comfortable with the old way of doing things. When someone gives me directions to a place, I pull out a pen and paper. When flying, while everyone else on the plane pulls out a laptop, I pull out my yellow legal pad. I've been taking care of business one way for so long that changing to a new way doesn't appeal to me.

That's the way many Christians respond to new directions in their lives. This is the way they view God's ability to bring about divine reversals. They look only at the previous way things were done and assume God has to stick to that plan.

But God has more plans than sand on the seashore. He has more ways than stars in the sky. God can reverse circumstances on a dime when He wants to. We need to learn how to trust and follow His leading. How to be open to His approach. And how to expect the unexpected, placing our hope in a God who isn't bound by time, tradition, or predictable paths. The closing chapters of Esther show us that our God is a God of reversals.

This week's teaching draws out themes found in Esther 7; 8; 9:20-27. Review these passages of Scripture before beginning your personal study.

◉ **DAY 1** ◉

THE SECOND BANQUET BEGINS

Just twenty-four hours had reset the stage. Haman, recently a happy man who thought he sat on top of the world, was now experiencing a Prozac® moment. He had just led his archenemy through the streets declaring that everyone must show him honor at the king's command. Haman's whole universe had been turned upside down, and he hadn't had time to figure out how to make it right again.

I'm sure Haman didn't feel like attending another banquet as a guest of Esther and her king, but the king's eunuchs came and escorted him there anyway (see Esth. 6:14). A reversal was about to take place.

How do you imagine Esther was feeling headed into this second banquet? How would her previous preparation help her be faithful in this tense, important moment?

According to Esther 7:1, what did the king and Haman do to begin the banquet with Esther? Why do you think Esther arranged things this way?

Esther knew her request was beyond what seemed humanly possible to grant. The king couldn't reverse his edict even if he wanted to. The laws that governed Persia were written in stone and couldn't be changed (see Dan. 6:15). She needed more than favor. She needed more than half of the kingdom. Esther needed a divine reversal of the devastation planned for her people. Therefore, Esther sought to make her king comfortable before sharing her need with him.

Record your view of what a divine reversal means in contemporary terms.

Esther obviously gave thought and planning to both the first and the second banquets. What steps are you taking right now in anticipation of God's faithfulness?

How does taking action help prepare us for God's eventual providence?

As the king, the queen, and Haman dined once again, the king extended his offer to Esther once more of up to half of the kingdom. It was a tempting offer on any other day, no doubt, but not on this day. Half of the kingdom would do little to secure the safety and survival of her people. Esther knew she needed more than this offer could provide, so she asked for her life and the lives of her people. Notice that she started with herself (see Esth. 7:3).

Why do you think Esther began by asking the king to spare her own life?

Read Esther 7:4. How did Esther present her argument so as to appeal to the king and his position?

This wasn't Esther's first rodeo. She knew what manner of man she was dealing with. Mere reason wouldn't work for this king. He was a leader of war, victory, power, and pride. Thus, Esther appealed to the king's sympathies and ego. First she stated that her own life was in jeopardy in order to capture his attention and bring the crisis closer to home. Next she shared that all of her people were at risk of annihilation, revealing that she was a Jew. Finally, she appealed to the king's pride by telling him they would all willingly be slaves to him without complaint. But if he would be so kind, she asked him to spare their lives.

Notice that Esther didn't start with an accusation. She didn't blame Haman. She didn't offer evidence she had found about him. She didn't seek to elevate Mordecai for saving the king's life. These approaches might seem logical to us because they emanate from the sense of truth and justice in our souls. But sometimes the way to move people isn't through an appeal to truth or justice but to their own needs. Esther's king needed to feel honored. He needed to feel respected. He needed to feel in control. Esther was wise enough to know these facts and to phrase her request in the most persuasive language and tone.

Have you experienced a divine reversal in your life? Explain.

If you're waiting for a divine reversal, what's one action step you can take this week as you wait?

✶ PRAYER ✶

Faithful God, give me wisdom as I face people and situations in my life that resist the forward progress You've planned for me. Grace my lips with wise persuasion, as Your Word says in Proverbs 16:23-24. In Christ's name, amen.

TIMING IS EVERYTHING

Esther finally made her request. She asked the king to spare her life and the lives of her people. The king was shocked, confused, and alarmed all at once. He asked Esther who created such a terrible plan to harm her and her people. That's when she turned her attention to Haman. "A foe and an enemy is this wicked Haman!" Esther responded (Esth. 7:6), no doubt unsure as to the king's loyalty toward his secondhand man. Esther didn't have the years of camaraderie that Haman had established with the king. She could see him only when invited. And now she was accusing one of his drinking buddies. How would the king react?

Esther had risked all to accuse the king's best friend, but it was her only option. And God had already revealed the crack in his character through the reading of the chronicles and the honoring of Mordecai. Maybe that would be enough to raise a question mark in the king's mind.

Because God had waited to release Esther to tell the king until the time was right, the king didn't even question her. Rather, he immediately became enraged. Scripture tells us that he stormed out into the palace gardens (see v. 7).

> **Review Esther 7:2-10. Take a moment to consider the importance of the timing of this revelation. How different might the king's reaction have been if Esther had accused Haman the first time she entered the king's court? How different might his reaction have been if she had accused him at the first banquet?**

> **What do we learn from this account about God's timing and character?**

This account shows us the value of patience and discernment when waiting for God's timing of events, conversations, and actions in our lives. Only God knows the perfect timing for events to take place. It may seem that it's taking too long according to our own schedule, but God's schedule is perfect. Trusting Him and His leading will enable us to move forward at the perfect time for His plan to take place.

Read the following verse.

> *The vision is yet for the appointed time;*
> *It hastens toward the goal and it will not fail.*
> *Though it tarries, wait for it;*
> *For it will certainly come, it will not delay.*
> HABAKKUK 2:3

What does this verse tell us about God's timing?

When do you struggle waiting for God? What are some things you do to remind yourself that He's worth waiting for?

Do you think most Christians realize the critical importance of waiting for God's timing? Why or why not?

It's easy in our fast-paced, get-it-now culture to become impatient as God lays out His plan. In our instant-gratification society, waiting has become a lost art. However, if Esther had asked the king for mercy for herself and her people before God had set the stage, she may have faced a different result. Rushing ahead of God is always a mistake.

Read Psalm 27:14. What does it mean to "be strong and let your heart take courage" as you wait?

According to Galatians 6:9, what are we waiting for when we remain obedient and faithful to God?

In what ways does God reward our patience when we wait for His timing?

While the king was outside trying to get a grip on his emotions, Haman foolishly approached Esther to beg for his life. Yet timing came into play once again. Just at that moment the king returned:

> When the king returned from the palace garden into the
> place where they were drinking wine, Haman was falling
> on the couch where Esther was. Then the king said, "Will he
> even assault the queen with me in the house?" As the word
> went out of the king's mouth, they covered Haman's face.
> ESTHER 7:8

As the king saw this scene, still hot from his rage, I imagine he had to be thinking, *You've got to be kidding me! Haman, you already want to kill my wife, and now you're assaulting her in my own home!* If the king's hatred for Haman hadn't reached full capacity before he went outside, it was beyond the boiling point when he returned.

Understand that Haman wasn't actually assaulting Esther. He was begging for his life. In an ironic twist Haman was falsely accused, just as Haman had falsely accused the Jews. The king's rage determined Haman's fate. Immediately the king's servants covered Haman's face, not allowing him even a moment to speak for himself. Working through the impression that had been created, God didn't provide an opportunity for Haman to defend himself. When God acts in judgment against an enemy of His will, He often acts swiftly.

What did the eunuchs suggest after they covered Haman's face (see Esth. 7:9)?

Recall a time when God reversed a situation for you or someone you know. How did His work affect your faith?

God had delayed Esther from telling the king the first two times he had asked what she wanted from him. If Esther had impulsively gone ahead of God's timing, Haman wouldn't have become angry at Mordecai and wouldn't have built the gallows on which he would now be hanged. Esther's obedience to God's divine timing allowed Haman to dig his own grave.

God allows unbelievers or enemies of His will to express their anger so that He can use it to stop the person from carrying out destruction. It's all about timing. God is a God of reversals. When the right time comes in His sovereign plan, He can quickly reverse things that appear to be irreversible.

✳ PRAYER ✳

Lord, I desire greater patience and deeper discernment
in following Your leading in my life. Give me rest when
worry disturbs me. Give me peace whe. concerns affect my
thinking. I choose to place my hope in You, knowing that in Your
perfect timing You can turn things around. In Christ's name, amen.

⊙ DAY 3 ⊙

THE GOD OF REVERSALS

As you complete this Bible study, maybe you're waiting for God to reverse a situation in your life, to turn things around, to vindicate you, or to remove the person who stands in your way. Perhaps you're in an unfair job situation or a family member isn't treating you with love. Maybe someone is jealous of you and seeks to belittle you to others, and you see no way to stop them. You may be facing a financial crisis or a health challenge.

You aren't alone. We all look to God to reverse many harmful or troubling situations in our lives. I want to remind you that God can change your circumstances with the flip of a switch. You may think your boss has the final say. You may think the powers that be have the final say. You may think the unscrupulous coworkers who are plotting against you have the final say. You may think because other people have a name, money, a position, or power that what they say goes. But the truth is, they don't anything unless God gives it to them. Furthermore, the God who gives it can also take it away.

Read Daniel 4:30. What does this verse tell you about King Nebuchadnezzar's heart and mind?

In what ways did the king's heart and mind contradict God's truth?

Now read Daniel 4:31-36. What were the results of God's intervention in this king's life? What lessons did he learn?

If God can reverse the seemingly supreme power of a king in an instant, is the opposition of anything or anyone too difficult for Him to overcome? The answer to that is a resounding no. You may not be able to see the way He will do it, but you must trust that He's in the process of doing it as you remain obedient to Him in your thoughts and actions.

The overarching principle behind God's power to bring about a divine reversal is simple: there's only one source of authority. If you can ever plant this truth deep in your heart, in the very center of your being, you'll be set free from worry, stress, and anger. No human being, no matter who they are, has the final authority over you as a Christian who lives by the Spirit in the will of God. Nobody.

This means you never have to live afraid. You never have to live threatened. Things may look threatening to you, but you never have to view them as they look because no human has the final say. God does.

In what ways does this truth set you free from worry or fear?

Identify a time when another person was exercising control over you in a detrimental way and God turned the situation around for you. What did you learn from this experience?

Why is it important to keep your life free from worry and anger, especially when you want God to intervene and turn a circumstance around?

Read Romans 12:19. What does it mean to "leave room for the wrath of God"?

Being vengeful isn't helpful. When you store up anger, revenge, jealousy, and other sinful thoughts and emotions, you aren't leaving room for God's wrath. Instead, you're placing distance between yourself and God and from your potential solution. Jesus said we should love our enemies (see Matt. 5:44). Always treat others with kindness, respect, and authentic love that stem from the conviction that God sees when others wrong you. He desires to turn your circumstance around. He can intervene if you'll step back, swallow your difficult emotions, and remain obedient to Him in all you do.

What lessons can we apply from Esther about enduring when we're called to suffer?

In what area of your life are you waiting for a divine reversal? Take a moment to ask God to reverse this circumstance in your life.

You may not know the way God will bring about a divine reversal in your situation, but you don't need to know. Trust His heart. Stay tethered to His love. Remain obedient to His Word. Follow His leading. Step out in faith. When you do, you'll see Him turn things around in a way you never could have imagined.

✳ PRAYER ✳

Lord, Your Word is truth. When I abide in Your Word and let love guide and guard my heart in Christ Jesus, I can witness Your hand move in ways I never imagined. Thank You for Your power and authority, which can bring about divine reversals in my life. In Christ's name, amen.

PERSONAL RESPONSIBILITY

God doesn't always work out our situation in ways we anticipate. The pathway to arriving at our purpose in life sometimes veers off in a direction we didn't know was possible. Esther and her people faced certain death. They also lived in a time when the king they served was unable to reverse his own decrees. So how could God spare Esther and her people from annihilation?

Although the king didn't have the power to revoke what he had already set in motion, he provided an alternative plan. He instructed his scribes to write letters authorizing the Jews to defend themselves against the attack on their lives. These letters were then dispersed among all the inhabitants in the land in time for them to plan their counterattack. In the legacy of the kings who had come before him and established certain rights for foreigners in the land, the king gave the Jewish people the right to defend themselves. This king thus empowered the people he had previously doomed. Empowerment often involves imparting knowledge, which is one of the greatest tools that can be given to people either to lift themselves out of or defend themselves in an unjust situation like the one faced by the Jews.

Read Esther 8:11-12. What did the king allow the Jews to do?

Describe the difference between empowerment and entitlement. What principles can we apply today in seeking to lift others from destructive circumstances?

Often when we read the story of Esther, we view her as a heroine who rescued her people from certain death. However, I hope you've seen through this study that Esther didn't rescue her people from certain death at all. She didn't demand that the king cancel his edict. She didn't reverse the decree. She merely enabled her people to defend themselves from the threat of certain death. And she enabled them through the knowledge of the upcoming battle, along with the right to bear arms.

What the Jews gained through Esther's stand was the knowledge of the ensuing battle, which allowed them the time to amass and use arms to legally defend themselves from their oppressors. Esther didn't win the battle for her people; she simply gave her people the ability to fight for themselves.

In what ways does the story of Esther demonstrate the importance of personal responsibility in overcoming challenges?

How can we surrender to and trust in God's activity while also exercising personal responsibility in our actions?

Read the following verse.

> *It is God who is at work in you, both to will and to work for His good pleasure.*
> PHILIPPIANS 2:13

How does this verse reflect the importance of waiting on God and moving according to His direction?

God is at work in you both to will and to work out His plan. He provides the motivation, direction, and leading you're to act on. Then you have the responsibility to act on what God has shown you. Waiting on God doesn't mean doing nothing. Esther fasted and prayed before entering the king's court, but she also followed God's leading to prepare a banquet. God leads as you seek Him. It's up to you to follow that leading on the pathway He has designed for you. When you do, you can see Him empower you, provide for you, protect you, and work in your situation, just as He did for the Jews.

God has an override button that nullifies even what Satan brings against you. People may align themselves against you, or circumstances may arise that aren't in your favor. But when God pushes the override button, He provides a way out. It may not stop others' evil from being evil, but it can cause that evil to boomerang and strike them instead so that you come out ahead when all is said and done. Isaiah 59:19 says:

> *When the enemy comes in like a flood,*
> *The Spirit of the* LORD *will lift up a standard against him.*
> ISAIAH 59:19, NKJV

God will push the override button. God will rise up with double the force.

What does it mean for the Holy Spirit to "lift up a standard" against His enemies?

Is there an area of your life in which you need to take more personal responsibility to follow what God has led you to do? Identify next steps you can take.

God is so good at turning circumstances around when you move in accordance with His leading that He can even heal your emotional wounds. Recall Esther 4:3:

> *There was great mourning among the Jews, with fasting,*
> *weeping and wailing; and many lay on sackcloth and ashes.*
> ESTHER 4:3

That was the scene when the first law was passed. But when the second law was passed and the carriers sent the message to the Jews that they could defend themselves, we read:

Pathways

For the Jews there was light and gladness and joy and honor.
In each and every province and in each and every city,
wherever the king's commandment and his decree arrived,
there was gladness and joy for the Jews, a feast and a holiday.
ESTHER 8:16-17

God can do the same for you. You may be crying today, but don't think that's how it's going to be when you wake up tomorrow. Not when God enters the situation. He can wipe away tears. He can turn pain into pleasure. He can turn sadness into joy.

Read the following verses.

"Hear, O LORD, and be gracious to me;
O LORD, be my helper."
You have turned for me my mourning into dancing;
You have loosed my sackcloth and girded me with gladness,
That my soul may sing praise to You and not be silent.
O LORD my God, I will give thanks to You forever.
PSALM 30:10-12

What does it mean for God to be our helper?

Read Jesus' words.

I tell you the truth, it is to your advantage that
I go away; for if I do not go away, the Helper will
not come to you; but if I go, I will send Him to you.
JOHN 16:7

Who's the helper described in this verse?

According to the psalmist, how is this help experienced in our lives?

Personal responsibility calls us to obey God in faith and lean into His will. It means we learn to listen for and recognize His voice and to submit to His will. John 16 describes the Holy Spirit the same way God is described in Psalm 30. God the Holy Spirit is our helper. He applies the benefits of our redemption to our soul so that we're joyful in the middle of hardship. He helps us operate according to His divine-reversal principle. As you submit to His leading and His timing and He intervenes in your situation, your emotions can change in an instant from despair to joy.

In what situation do you need to depend on the Holy Spirit this week?

✳ PRAYER ✳

Lord, I want to operate according to Your divine leading.
I want to align my thoughts, actions, and desires with Your own.
I know when I do, You'll intervene and bring about a divine
reversal in the challenges I'm facing. Thank You for all You're
about to do as I surrender to You. In Christ's name, amen.

⊙ DAY 5 ⊙

YOUR PATHWAY

Many days I wish I could be one of those preachers who tell people that if you come to God, you'll have no enemies; you'll face no difficult days; you'll have no lean years, disappointments, or bad employers. I wish I could preach that, but if I did, I would be lying. Throughout Scripture God allows challenges, setbacks, and negative scenarios because it's against the backdrop of impossibilities that His beauty shines through. Just as a diamond glistens most brightly when placed against a dark backdrop, God's glory displays brightly as He brings about divine reversals in the face of seemingly insurmountable obstacles.

Yes, you'll face challenges on the pathway to your purpose. But whatever you come up against, it doesn't need to have the last say. When you remain tethered to the One who pulls the strings, you can witness Him come through for you in every way.

Read Exodus 14 and summarize the way God intervened.

Read Matthew 14:13-21. In what way did God turn this situation around? What perspective did Jesus take into the challenge?

Why is it important to demonstrate trust in and gratitude to God in the face of difficulties?

If the Book of Esther has taught us anything, it has taught us to change our perspective. Perspective is the way we see what we see. Sometimes we can be surrounded by threatening circumstances that don't look good at all. But when we learn how to view life with a kingdom perspective, we recognize the positive side of every difficulty we face. With God there's always an upside. A challenge is simply an opportunity for Him to showcase His power in our lives.

The Red Sea didn't signify certain death for the Israelites as the Egyptians chased them in six hundred chariots armed for battle. No, the Red Sea was the stage on which God performed two miracles: parting the water for the people to pass and drying the ground so that they wouldn't get bogged down in the mud (see Ex. 14).

The fainting five thousand (not including women and children) who followed Jesus to hear Him teach weren't a humanitarian disaster waiting to happen. No, feeding the five thousand with bread crumbs and fish was the screen on which Jesus showcased His authority over the natural realm, as well as His character of trust and gratitude in the presence of need and want (see Matt. 14:13-21).

The planned annihilation of the Jews by a resentful, proud man named Haman wasn't the end of God's people, whom He had chosen to bless the world. No, it was the backdrop for a saga that highlighted His providential power to reverse events, decrees, and positions with ease and precision.

Studying the story of Esther will challenge anyone's perspective on luck. Divine providence and luck can't coexist. Chance, fate, and happenstance don't exist simultaneously with God's providential hand. The providence of God means God is in control by either causing or allowing all events.

Now that we've almost completed a study of God's *providence*, how would you define that term?

What's your opinion of luck now that you've almost finished this study?

The Book of Esther is designed to expand your view of God, to shift your perspective away from spotting the challenges and difficulties of life toward seeing the opportunities God has created to highlight His power. We've seen that nowhere in the entire Book of Esther is God's name mentioned. The fact that He's not overtly seen makes even more remarkable the results He brought about. And observing what He did in the story of Esther should make it easier for you to recognize His fingerprints in your life and in your circumstances, even though you can't visibly see Him. Nothing will free you from frustration, anxiety, and confusion like realizing the supreme sovereignty of God.

What are key principles or lessons you've learned in this study?

In what ways do you intend to apply what you've learned to your thoughts and actions? How have you already begun to apply what you've learned, and how have you experienced God's intervention in your circumstances?

When believers get off course from the pathway of purpose God has ordained for them, the problem isn't that God has failed to be God. The major problem is that we're misaligned with Him, so we react in the flesh and in our own power to the negative situations around us. Therefore, we miss seeing God and His activity.

Aligning yourself with Christ and His Word is key to experiencing the divine intervention you need in your life. You must abide in Him in order to be guided by Him and live according to His Word. When you do, you'll experience the direction you need to move further on the pathway where He has placed you.

Record ways John 15:5-8 connects with the principles we've learned by studying the life of Esther.

Read Esther 9:1-2. What was the result of God's divine intervention in Esther's life and the lives of her people?

**Make a commitment to memorize Romans 8:28 and 1 John 3:22.
Let these two verses settle deep in your soul and shape your emotions
and responses to life's challenges.**

Our God is a God of providence. Ultimately, it doesn't matter what others have done to you or what your finances, health, or circumstances are. They don't determine the resolution of your circumstance. Only God sets in motion the final course for your life. God designs the intersections on the pathway to your purpose.

Your responsibility as a Christian is to remain tied to God's Word and close to His Son, Jesus Christ, so that each step you take is the one He's guiding you to take. Step by step you'll reach your destination. Yes, some steps are harder than others. Some hills are steeper than others. Some treks are more treacherous than others. But all are necessary in getting you where God wants you to go. You don't have to see the destination when you set out on your journey. You just have to know the One who can. He will guide, direct, and sustain you as you stay close to Him every step along the path.

God knows the way. He knows the play. He's writing the script. He's setting the stage. He's changing the scenes. He's casting the characters. You just need to obey His direction as He guides you along the pathway to the grand, spectacular destiny He has ordained for you.

✳ PRAYER ✳

Lord, I love You. Thank You for the power of Your providence. Thank You for knowing the way I take and the best direction for me to travel. I trust and rest in You. I place my faith in You. I honor You with my entire heart for the goodness You're able to bring into every situation I face. Keep me on the pathway of Your divine purpose and let me bring glory to You and good to others. In Christ's name, amen.

STUDY START DATE

_____ / _____ / _____

✎ **Record a few details about this season of your life.**

FAMILY |

_____   _____
name   age

_____   _____

_____   _____

_____   _____

_____   _____

WORK |

_____
company

_____
position

HOME |

_____   _____
city   state

What do you hope to get out of this study?

hot

Mark your spiritual temperature.

cold

🌐 **MAJOR EVENTS IN THE WORLD** |

_____

_____

📍 **KEY ISSUES IN <u>YOUR</u> WORLD** |

_____

_____

STUDY END DATE

_____ / _____ / _____

★ **TOP FIVE FAVORITE POINTS FROM THIS STUDY**   *page #*

_____

_____

_____

_____

_____

**WHERE DID
YOU STUDY?**

○ Home

○ Church

○ Another home:
_____

○ Other:
_____

**WITH WHOM DID YOU
DO THIS STUDY?**

_____

_____

_____

_____

**WITH WHOM DO
YOU WANT TO SHARE
THIS STUDY?**

_____

BIBLE VERSES TO MEMORIZE

YOUR *Eternity* IS OUR *Priority*

At The Urban Alternative, eternity is our priority—for the individual, the family, the church and the nation. The 45-year teaching ministry of Tony Evans has allowed us to reach a world in need with:

The Alternative – Our flagship radio program brings hope and comfort to an audience of millions on over 1,300 radio outlets across the country.

tonyevans.org – Our library of teaching resources provides solid Bible teaching through the inspirational books and sermons of Tony Evans.

Tony Evans Training Center – Experience the adventure of God's Word with our online classroom, providing at-your-own-pace courses for your PC or mobile device.

Tony Evans app – Packed with audio and video clips, devotionals, Scripture readings and dozens of other tools, the mobile app provides inspiration on-the-go.

**Explore God's kingdom today.
Live for more than the moment.**
Live for *eternity.*

tonyevans.org

Also from
TONY EVANS

DETOURS
The Unpredictable Path to Your Destiny
6 sessions

Find hope in understanding that the sudden or seemingly endless detours in life are God's way of moving you from where you are to where He wants you to be.

Leader Kit 006104403
Bible Study Book 006104401

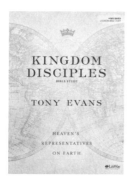

KINGDOM DISCIPLES
Heaven's Representatives on Earth
6 sessions

Develop a confidence and urgency to fulfill your primary responsibility to be a disciple and to make other disciples.

Leader Kit 005469850
Bible Study Book 005469851

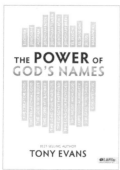

THE POWER OF GOD'S NAMES
6 sessions

Learn the meanings of God's names to know Him more fully and experience Him more deeply.

Leader Kit 005634204
Member Book 005634003

LifeWay.com/TonyEvans | 800.458.2772 | LifeWay Christian Stores
Pricing and availability subject to change without notice.

LifeWay